Literacy
Beyond
Picture Books

Teaching
Secondary
Students with
Moderate
to Severe
Disabilities

Dorothy Dendy Smith
Jill Fisher DeMarco
Martha Worley

CORWIN
A SAGE Company

For information:

Corwin
A SAGE Company
2455 Teller Road
Thousand Oaks, California 91320
(800) 233-9936
Fax: (800) 417-2466
www.corwinpress.com

SAGE Ltd.
1 Oliver's Yard
55 City Road
London EC1Y 1SP
United Kingdom

SAGE Pvt. Ltd.
B 1/I 1 Mohan Cooperative Industrial Area
Mathura Road, New Delhi 110 044
India

SAGE Asia-Pacific Pte. Ltd.
33 Pekin Street #02-01
Far East Square
Singapore 048763

Printed in the United States of America

Library of Congress Cataloging-in-Publication Data

Smith, Dorothy Dendy.
Literacy beyond picture books: teaching secondary students with moderate to severe disabilities/Dorothy Dendy Smith, Jill Fisher DeMarco, Martha Worley.
    p. cm.
Includes bibliographical references and index.
ISBN 978-1-4129-7113-3 (cloth)
ISBN 978-1-4129-7114-0 (pbk.)

    1. Children with mental disabilities—Education (Secondary) 2. Language arts—Remedial teaching. 3. Literature—Study and teaching (Secondary) I. DeMarco, Jill Fisher. II. Worley, Martha. III. Title.

LC4604.S65 2009
371.9'0473—dc22   2008054789

This book is printed on acid-free paper.

09 10 11 12 13   10 9 8 7 6 5 4 3 2 1

Acquisitions Editor:	Carol Chambers Collins
Editorial Assistant:	Brett Ory
Production Editor:	Veronica Stapleton
Copy Editor:	Adam Dunham
Typesetter:	C&M Digitals (P) Ltd.
Proofreader:	Caryne Brown
Indexer:	Sheila Bodell
Cover Designer:	Rose Storey
Graphic Designer:	Karine Hovsepian

Contents

List of Photographs   vi

List of Tables and Figures   viii

Foreword   ix
    Karena Cooper-Duffy

Acknowledgments   xii

About the Authors   xiv

Introduction: A Quest for Change   1
    The Way We Were   1
    Increased Awareness   1
    Parent Lobbying   2
    Government Mandates   2
    Program Development   2

1.   **Research and Program Overview**   4
    Research   4
    Program Overview, Premise, and Goal   9
    Program Principles   9

2.   **Establishing a Foundation for Planning**   11
    Teacher Objectives   11
    Basic Planning Principles   12
    Understanding the Students   12
    Team Approach   14
    Thematic Approach   18
    The Use of Age-Appropriate Literature   19
    Technology   21

3.   **Building a Theme**   23
    Teacher Objectives   23
    Choosing a Theme Concept   23

Choosing a Book 25
Planning 26
Finalizing Plans 29
Scheduling Events 30
Parent Communication 30
Additional Planning Aids 33
Building a Theme: A Checklist 34

4. Setting the Stage **35**
Teacher Objectives 35
Providing Structure 35
Structuring the Classroom Environment 36
Structuring Activities 36
Scheduling 37
Enhancement of the Classroom Environment 39
Providing Materials for Hands-On Learning 41
Preparing Technology 43
Other Classroom Materials 45
Setting the Stage: A Checklist 46

5. Providing Access Through Assistive Technology **47**
Teacher Objectives 47
Assistive Technology 47
Technology in Our Program 53

6. Instructional Delivery **57**
Teacher Objectives 57
Theme Introduction 57
Introducing Vocabulary 59
Sharing the Literature Chapter-by-Chapter 60
Retelling 60
Retelling Questions for Chapter 3, "Willy Drives the Herd" . 64
Teaching Vocabulary 67
Guided Reading 69
Building Language 71
Community Experiences 72
Predictable Chart Writing 72
Within the School: How We Bring Literature to Life 74
Presentations 77
Advanced Assignments 77
Concluding a Theme 79
Instructional Delivery: A Checklist 80

7. **Home Involvement**   **81**
   Teacher Objectives   81
   Sharing the Retelling   82
   Sharing the Vocabulary   82
   Presentations   83
   Home Involvement: A Checklist   84

8. **Assessment**   **85**
   Teacher Objectives   85
   Individual Journaling   85
   Addressing the Standard Course of Study   87
   Data Collection   88
   Graphing   92
   Retelling as Assessment   94
   Adaptive Programs   94
   Games   94
   Assessment: A Checklist   97

9. **Inclusion and Collaboration With General Education Teachers** **99**
   Teacher Objective   99
   Special Education Teachers Working With
       General Education Teachers   100
   Peer Tutors   102
   General Education: A Checklist   103

10. **Functional Skills**   **104**
    Teacher Objective   104
    Teaching Skills Throughout the Day   104

Sample Lesson Plans and Related Resources   **106**

Web Resources for Literacy Support   **187**

Glossary   **189**

References   **193**

Index   **196**

List of Photographs

CHAPTER 4

Photo 4.1 A bulletin board designed to
build excitement as a theme is launched 39

Photo 4.2 Vocabulary display in theme area 40

Photo 4.3 A mural from *The Wizard of Oz* 41

Photo 4.4 Student work showing both artwork and
written-expression opportunities 42

Photo 4.5 A theme-related math lesson in which
students graphed birth months 43

CHAPTER 5

Photo 5.1 An IntelliTools keyboard used for written expression 49

Photo 5.2 Adapted communication notebook
providing continuous access to vocabulary words 54

Photo 5.3 Communication notebook with words only for a
more advanced student 55

Photo 5.4 An adapted communication page designed to
assist with accessibility needs 56

Photo 5.5 An Intellikeys overlay for the Internet when learning
about the Iditarod during a theme based on *Stone Fox* 56

CHAPTER 6

Photo 6.1 A chart showing a recorded retelling,
math skills, highlighting of the consonant P,
and sharing the pen 61

Photo 6.2 Communication notebook showing QWERTY keyboard 63

Photo 6.3 Retelling of Chapter 11 in *The Whale Rider*. Note "sharing
the pen" for "got," "to," "backs," "sides," and "keep"
and highlighted letters 65

Photo 6.4   Students looking for words during vocabulary lesson   68

Photo 6.5   Student identifying vocabulary word   69

Photo 6.6   Making our own constitution led to opportunities for teaching literacy skills when reading *The Jungle Book*   70

Photo 6.7   A winter outing to Krispy Kreme   72

Photo 6.8   Raising awareness of print through student-created books developed through predictable chart writing   73

Photo 6.9   Mr. Tumnus, a character from *The Lion, the Witch, and the Wardrobe*, helps bring literature to life in the classroom   74

Photo 6.10   Matthew Burrill, who portrayed Romey in *Where the Lilies Bloom*, answers questions from the students.   75

Photo 6.11   Staff and students hold an eighteenth-century feast after reading the many versions of *Cinderella*   75

Photo 6.12   A student dressed as *The Neverending Story* character Teeny Weeny   76

Photo 6.13   Students enjoy a belly dancer during a reading of *Aladdin*   76

Photo 6.14   Student making a presentation about arctic animals during a theme based on *Stone Fox*   78

Photo 6.15   Student making a presentation on bananas during a theme based on *The Jungle Book*   78

Photo 6.16   End of theme celebration: a cookie made by Lewis   80

CHAPTER 8

Photo 8.1   A student's demonstration of emergent literacy skills shown by writing M's for flying monkeys from *The Wizard of Oz*   86

Photo 8.2   A student's demonstration of the awareness of print following the reading of a chapter from *Heidi*   86

Photo 8.3   Journaling demonstrating more advanced written expression and comprehension   86

Photos 8.4 and 8.5   Matching vocabulary to books in a group comprehension lesson. This activity demonstrated retention of vocabulary and the connection to literature selections covered over the course of one school year.   96

Photo 8.6   Students show comprehension through a Venn diagram comparing *The Wizard of Oz* and *The Lion, the Witch, and the Wardrobe*.   97

CHAPTER 9

Photo 9.1   A peer tutor and a student practice reading a predictable chart page   103

List of Tables and Figures

CHAPTER 2

Table 2.1   Challenges/Implications and Solutions: Ways in Which
Thematic Instruction, Age-Appropriate Literature and
Technology Aid Students in Overcoming Challenges   22

CHAPTER 3

Figure 3.1   Thematic Unit Planning Sheet (Graphic Organizer
or Planning Web)   27

CHAPTER 4

Table 4.1   Weekly Schedule   38

CHAPTER 5

Table 5.1   Technology Vendors   51

CHAPTER 6

Table 6.1   Retelling of Chapter 3 of *Stone Fox*, "Willy Drives
the Herd"   64

CHAPTER 8

Table 8.1   IEP Goals Data Sheet for Letters   89
Table 8.2   IEP Goals Data Sheet for Vocabulary   90
Table 8.3   IEP Goals Data Sheet for Comprehension Questions   91
Table 8.4   IEP Goals Data Sheet for Math   93

Foreword

This book is a treasure chest packed full of beautiful, radiant, and rare gems that teachers can use to uncover the sparkling abilities of children with significant intellectual disabilities.

AUTHORS

The authors of this book are three of the most talented and creative professionals, who together initiated an innovative, effective, and cutting edge approach to teaching literacy to children with significant intellectual disabilities. These three authors work under the motto, "What will it take for this student to effectively enjoy and master this material?" They never state, "This child is too disabled to learn, so why bother teaching him." They are always searching for new ideas and methods to bring into the classroom to enhance a student's understanding of the information. Even more remarkable, these ladies are some of the most selfless people: They share their lesson plans, ideas, resources, assistive devices, and all materials with anyone who asks for assistance, so that other teachers do not waste their time struggling to teach. This team also invests numerous hours each year providing guest lectures in college courses and supervising special education interns from several local universities. I see this book as the next phase of their work in the field. It is a way to reach out to other educators who are just starting out and to educators who are struggling alone to meet the legal and ethical requirements of teaching literacy to children with significant intellectual disabilities. These authors are all too aware of the high turnover rate of special education teachers. They are not only supporting the children but they are also trying to revive the passion and creativity that so many teachers in special education have lost. Teaching does require that many legal mandates are met, but it can be done with a magic wand in one hand, a pair of ruby slippers on your feet, and a bag of tricks that hold all the children in high anticipation.

SPECIAL CONTRIBUTIONS

This book is written in a user-friendly way that is free of jargon and unnecessary technical language. It begins with a brief overview of the research literature on teaching literacy to children with significant intellectual disabilities. The literature is summarized and then used to describe how research-based strategies can be interwoven into practical daily instruction plans. Each chapter describes in great detail how to plan and implement strategies for teaching literacy to children who have significant intellectual disabilities and are unable to actively participate in group instruction. The authors address the realities they face when teaching children with challenging behaviors, significant intellectual disabilities, and no exposure to literature. The chapters have superior examples of everything from what the thematic lesson should look like, how to adapt vocabulary sheets, how to embed assistive technology, how to create assessment tools to evaluate the learner's comprehension, and how to create homework assignments. These examples can be recreated easily.

The key element embedded through the book is the importance of collaboration with numerous people throughout each thematic unit. The book contains numerous ideas of people critical to work with, such as the school librarian, general education teachers, therapists, parents and many others. There are also guidelines for facilitating positive collaboration. In several instances, the authors have provided examples of possible scenarios that may occur while collaborating with others and how to handle those situations.

AUDIENCE

This book is designed for special education and general education teachers interested in working collaboratively to create exciting, effective literacy experiences for students with significant intellectual disabilities. It is a great tool for special education teachers who are just starting out in the field and are looking for a roadmap to begin exploring ways to connect daily instruction to the standard course of study. It is also a handy resource for experienced teachers frustrated with the endless list of new requirements imposed on special education teachers. This resource provides experienced teachers of all levels with a variety of examples to expand, refresh, and rejuvenate current instruction with new approaches to teaching literacy to heterogeneous groups of learners with significant intellectual disabilities.

ULTIMATE SIGNIFICANCE OF THE BOOK

After working with the authors for the last 10 years, watching them teach, and reading their work, I can honestly say that this book is a guide to planning unique, student-focused lessons that can lead to student mastery of age-appropriate literature. The authors stated on numerous occasions, "We won't know how much students can learn until we teach them in a way they can understand." I watched students arrive at middle school with no exposure to academic material and within a few months they were sitting in a group (without challenging behavior), actively participating in literacy activities. The students were listening to age-appropriate books (for more than 15 minutes), watching the literature come to life through a video, spelling words, writing sentences with adapted pencils or word cards and pictures, answering complex comprehension questions related to the stories, and using new vocabulary throughout their school day. I was so excited about these teaching strategies that I designed my own thematic unit and had to try it myself. The students loved the unit, and I loved teaching it.

Dr. Karena Cooper-Duffy
Associate Professor in Special Education
Western Carolina University

Acknowledgments

First of all, we would like to thank our students and their families for providing never-ending inspiration.

A special thanks to our own families for their patience, caring, and enthusiastic support, including the provision of comfort food and respite during times of intense work. Thanks to Dixie Fisher (Jill's mother) and Genny Bryant for lending expertise in the form of editing. Thanks to Martha and Jay Tolar for providing a relaxing, distraction free, and supportive place to work at the Top of the Forest.

Thanks to the following individuals in Buncombe County Schools: our team members, including our classroom assistants, fellow teachers, and related services personnel. Dr. Lin Moore supported us when the ideas for this book were new, and Norm Bossert continually encouraged us to raise the bar. Lee Crisp and David Thompson offered support, acknowledgement, and encouragement. In addition, we thank our current administrators, especially Jana Griggs, Brenda Simpson-Taylor, Thomas Keever, Jenny Klein, and Chloette Kuhlman.

Thanks to the North Carolina Center for the Advancement of Teaching (NCCAT) for providing an opportunity for creative work and the launching of this project during a wonderful week at the Teacher-Scholar-in-Residence Program.

Thanks to Western Carolina University for leading us to a new level of understanding of individuals with special needs, and especially Dr. Karena Cooper-Duffy.

A special thanks to Dr. Dennis Reid, who led us to believe that writing a book was possible and walked with us through the process.

PUBLISHER'S ACKNOWLEDGMENTS

Corwin gratefully acknowledges the contributions of the following reviewers:

Kimberly Bright, PhD
Associate Professor of Educational
   Leadership and Special Education
Shippensburg University
Shippensburg, PA

Erin Jones, MS SPED
Special Education Teacher
Tea, SD

Sharon Judge
Associate Dean
Old Dominion University
Norfolk, VA

Jayne Englert-Burns
Consulting Teacher, Special
   Education
Montgomery County Public Schools
Germantown, MD

Karen Kozy-Landress
NBCT, MEd, MA, CCC-SLP
Speech/Language Pathologist
Merritt Island, FL

Wendy Dallman
Special Education Teacher
New London High School
New London, WI

G. Richmond Mancil, PhD
Assistant Professor/Assistant
   Director
Western Kentucky University/
   Kelly Autism Program
Bowling Green, KY

Vicki Edwards
Director of Assessment and
   Student Achievement
Deer Valley Unified School District
Phoenix, AZ

Michelle Strom, NBCT
Language Arts Teacher
Carson Middle School
Fort Carson, CO

Lyman Goding
Lecturer, Secondary Education,
   Bridgewater (MA)
State College Principal (Retired),
   Plymouth Community (MA)
   Intermediate School
Bridgewater State College
Bridgewater, MA

About the Authors

 **Dorothy Dendy Smith** has taught in the field of special education for 27 years. She graduated from Western Carolina University in 1972 with a bachelor of science degree in special education. She received a master of arts in education, special education, severe disabilities, from Western Carolina in 2002. She has certifications in learning disabilities, mental retardation, and severe disabilities. She was Special Educator of Excellence for Buncombe County Schools for the 2006–2007 school year and Teacher of the Year for the Progressive Education Program in Buncombe County Schools for the year 2001–2002. She was the Teacher of the Year for Walnut Cove Primary School and First Runner-Up for Teacher of the Year in the Stokes County School District in North Carolina. She is currently the Autism Specialist for Buncombe County Schools. She lives in Black Mountain, North Carolina, and has two adult sons, a daughter-in-law, and two grandchildren.

 **Jill Fisher DeMarco** worked with adults with disabilities for 15 years before beginning her career in special education. She has a bachelor of science degree in vocational rehabilitation from Appalachian State University, a master of arts in teaching and a master of science degree in human resources from Western Carolina University. She has certifications in mental retardation and learning disabilities. She has taught high-school students in the Occupational Course of Study and currently is in the seventh year of teaching at the Progressive Education Program at Valley Springs Middle School in Arden, North Carolina. She was the 2005–2006 Teacher of the Year for the program. She and her husband live in Arden with their son and daughter.

 **Martha Worley** has a bachelor of arts from Baylor University and a master of science degree from Vanderbilt University. She has taught for 15 years in the public schools as a speech pathologist. She is currently a speech pathologist at the Progressive Education Program at Roberson High School in Asheville, North Carolina. She also works with other schools in Buncombe County to provide access to communication systems for students with significant communication needs. She was the Special Education Teacher of Excellence for Buncombe County Schools in the 2001–2002 school year. She lives with her husband in Asheville, North Carolina, and they have two daughters, a son-in-law, and three grandchildren: Jackson, Hannah, and Lucy.

Dorothy, Jill, and Martha have conducted workshops at the local and state levels, including the Council on Exceptional Children's Conference for the state of North Carolina. Dotty and Jill have worked closely with Western Carolina University by conducting training for students and supervising student teachers.

The authors may be reached at LiteracyBeyondPictureBooks@ Hotmail.com and www.LiteracyBeyondPictureBooks.com.

*This book is dedicated to Lacy, who brought
us joy and inspiration, and to Char, who always believed in us.*

Introduction

A Quest for Change

It could be argued with a good deal of persuasiveness that when one looks over the history of man the most distinguishing characteristic of his development is the degree to which man has underestimated the potentialities of men.

—Seymour Sarason, quoted in *Christmas in Purgatory*

THE WAY WE WERE

This book is the result of a process begun several years ago. Although our curriculum was adequate, we felt the need for improvement. Parent lobbying, concerns for quality of life, and government mandates were among the influences leading to a quest for change.

Our typical classroom schedule included story time, independent work sessions, self-help skills, group time, and special activities. Story time was based on juvenile materials, the work was repetitive and not productive, and skills for independent living were taught through multiple trials. Resources for providing excellent instruction were within reach, but not utilized in the most effective manner.

INCREASED AWARENESS

During 2000 to 2001, a number of influences began to lead to change. Through an excellent graduate program in severe disabilities at Western Carolina University, we were exposed to new ways of thinking about the rights and abilities of individuals with special needs. As we learned that

1

improved quality of life can improve behavior and that students with special needs should be taught using age-appropriate materials, we began to consider ways to improve our instructional program. We became increasingly aware of augmentative and alternative methods of communication and the promise they held for improving the lives of many students with special needs.

PARENT LOBBYING

At the same time we were becoming aware of the need for an improved quality of life, parents were exerting influence by lobbying for change. Many of our students' parents had broad visions for their children. They were advocating age-appropriate programs and rich educational opportunities. When these visions became missions, change began. Our parents played an important part in planting seeds of discontent with the way things were and in painting visions of meaningful instruction for children with special needs.

GOVERNMENT MANDATES

In addition to our heightened consciousness concerning the need for change, another altering force appeared. The Federal Government, through No Child Left Behind, began to demand that students with special needs be tested in language arts and math. Although there are issues with the No Child Left Behind program, and much more research and appropriate development are needed, the requirements presented a vehicle for change. This was the first time in history that students with significant cognitive disabilities were required to achieve in academic subjects linked to the standard course of study.

PROGRAM DEVELOPMENT

Realizing the need for a meaningful, interconnected, and age-appropriate program, we began to look for ways to give our students opportunities similar to those of their general education counterparts. Among the first steps in the planning of our program was the examination of published research. We also focused on listening to and talking with experts in the field of special education and literacy instruction.

Through the examination of research and literature and our discussions with experts, we realized that the struggle with how to help students with significant disabilities in the attainment of literacy skills is not new. The special learning needs of these students present a challenge in the quest to match need to methods to materials.

Difficulty with synthesis and retention of information, organizational difficulties, and delayed language are among the special learning characteristics impacting skills acquisition for students with significant disabilities. In addition, these students face challenges due to communication difficulties, sensory and physical impairments, and limited opportunities for experiences.

The search for resources led us to realize that few exist. This shortage of age-appropriate materials brought about the creation of our own program.

As we examined our own beliefs, we concluded that our program should be student centered and fully developed in content and experiences. We also determined that our program should be based on the use of meaningful age-appropriate materials and incorporate language arts instruction across all areas of the curriculum.

In an article discussing approaches to teaching reading, such as whole language or phonics, Cromwell (1997) verifies our decision as she states,

> The majority of experts now contend that neither approach by itself is effective all the time but that both approaches possess merit. What does succeed then, many experts say, is a carefully designed reading program that employs part phonics, and takes into account each students learning style and demonstrated strengths and weaknesses. (p. 4)

We are convinced that after years of struggling with how to teach literacy skills to middle- and high-school-age students with disabilities, an answer has been discovered.

Our program is an exciting work in progress. Our days are filled with wonderful learning opportunities for enthusiastic students with significant disabilities who are exceeding expectations. They are learning to learn, which is leading to new depths of understanding and the acquisition of skills once considered beyond their level of capability.

1 Research and Program Overview

RESEARCH

The teaching of age-appropriate literacy skills in the instruction of secondary-level students with significant disabilities is a relatively new area of interest for those in the field of special education. For many years, individuals with significant disabilities were not taught to read, or were taught through a variety of unsuccessful means. In the past, students with disabilities were often taught sight and functional/safety words. While this was beneficial, "real" literature, such as age-appropriate novels and poems—literature that is used in general education—was not often seen as an option for poor readers or nonreaders. Limited research is also available in this area.

In a review of studies by Browder, Wakeman, Spooner, Ahlgrim-Delzell, and Algozzine (2006) dealing with reading instruction and students with significant cognitive disabilities, it was found that most of the studies done in this area involved functional sight word acquisition and picture identification. Very few studies involved comprehension, phonics instruction, or phonemic awareness.

Our goal was to help our students improve their literacy skills and have accessibility to literature, so different methods for increasing our students' access to literature were researched. Any technique that could help students learn words and develop reading skills would be looked at and tried to see if it was helpful for the students. We felt the access to literature and words provided students in special education should equal that provided to students in a general education program.

When the search for information on the topic of teaching age-appropriate literature to students with disabilities began, current research and best practices were reviewed. At first, we were overwhelmed by the information. A Google search of "teaching reading to students with disabilities" yielded 8,470,000 results. After reviewing the "hits," it was found that the vast majority of the articles were about students with varying degrees of learning disabilities. There were also many lesson plans with accommodations for students with disabilities.

At this point, we needed a more specific definition of the population of students with whom we were working. Our classrooms are described as having students with intellectual disabilities. Our state recognizes the standard range for IQ levels of 52–68 for mild, 36–51 for moderate, 20–35 for severe, and below 20 for profound intellectual disability. The Merck Manual Online Medical Library (see Sulkes, 2006) describes the ranges of mental retardation and intellectual disability as needing different levels of support.

> Support is categorized as intermittent, limited, extensive, or pervasive. Intermittent means occasional support; limited means support such as a day program in a sheltered workshop; extensive means daily, ongoing support; and pervasive means a high level of support for all activities of daily living. (para. 4)

Other areas of eligibility in our classrooms include multihandicapped, autism, and other health impaired. Every student has his or her individual strengths and needs, but for the sake of a consistent definition—so you will know what our students "look like"—the IQ categories, moderate to severe, and the levels of support, from limited to extensive, will be used.

Next, a narrower Internet search using "reading and students with mental retardation" was done. Out of those results, most were textbooks, definitions of mental retardation, or aimed at teaching life skills. Finally, searching for "teaching age-appropriate literature to students with mental retardation" generally resulted in college catalogs with class descriptions and more definitions of mental retardation. There were not many articles that included step-by-step instructions on how to do the type of teaching we were hoping to do.

Since more academic findings and current research would be more helpful, a search was done through the Hunter Library at Western Carolina University and Ramsey Library at the University of North Carolina at Asheville. Research was done using a wide variety of journals. They included *Journal of Special Education, Remedial & Special Education, Learning Disabilities Research & Practice, Education & Treatment of Children, Child Language Teaching and Therapy,* and *Learning Disability Quarterly.*

We were surprised to find there were not many articles on the topic. Using the Academic Search Premier, "reading and students with disabilities" yielded 296 results but "teaching reading to students with severe disabilities" yielded 0. "Improving literacy skills" yielded 9, and "reading and students with mental retardation" yielded 5. A couple of things became evident to us: there was not a wealth of information available to us, and we were going to have to develop our own way of teaching and assessing that worked with our population of students.

Selection Criteria

For this review, certain criteria for each study were required.

1. A study needed a publication date after 1990. This criterion was chosen to assure more current information and best practices.

2. The studies had to be empirically based or a review of empirically based research.

3. The studies needed to deal with students who were considered to have moderate to severe disabilities. The students in the studies had to be receiving special education services.

4. The studies had to deal with strategies for increasing reading skills.

The results of the review of literature indicated there are many different ways to approach the teaching of reading to students with disabilities.

Curriculum-based measurement (CBM) is the basis for two studies (Allinder, 2000; Stecker & Fuchs, 2000). While more an assessment method than a teaching method, CBM is a data-based assessment that helps "monitor progress of individual students on an ongoing basis, determine what to teach, quickly determine if instruction is effective so that necessary changes in instruction can be made, and write measurable individual education goals" (Scott & Weishaar, 2003, p. 154). Both Allinder and Stecker and Fuchs looked at the effect curriculum-based measurement had on student progress. Both also used teachers who were teaching students with disabilities. The findings in their studies were similar. Students who have teachers who monitor the CBM and revise their instructional plans according to their students' needs progress at a faster rate than those whose teachers do not.

Specific techniques for increasing literacy skills for students with significant disabilities were discussed in five of the articles: Basil and Reyes (2003), Browder and Cooper-Duffy (2003), Collins and Griffen

(1996), Faykus and McCurdy (1998), and Winterling (1990). Among the techniques discussed were a computer program with teacher assistance, least intensive prompts, oral fluency, token reinforcement, and time delay. The computer program increased literacy skills, and token reinforcement combined with other techniques helped with word recognition. Time delay was found to be a good tool in teaching reading skills and improving progress. This tool helped show progress in the comprehension of sight words and safety-related issues concerning warning labels.

Morocco, Hindin, Mata-Aguilar, and Clark-Chiarelli (2001) evaluated a program designed to improve literacy skills for students with disabilities. The program was designed for students with and without disabilities using cooperative learning and peer tutoring. The students were involved in phases of learning that began with teacher instruction and ended with the students writing about their understanding of the literature. Age-level materials and activities designed to increase comprehension of the materials were used.

To read about the literacy program was very exciting. For too long, teachers in special education have limited their students to simple, often non-age-appropriate literature. They have looked only at the reading level rather than the whole process of understanding literature. This study shows that not only can students learn and benefit from literature programs; they can work with their peers and grow in their comprehension and appreciation for literature.

After looking at the research, we discussed different ways to increase reading and literacy skills. We really liked reading about the literacy program. One of us had taught using a similar thematic approach with elementary school students for many years. We decided to look into the theme approach to see if that way of teaching would benefit our students.

A basic definition of theme teaching is that it "involves creating an array of activities around a central idea. These activities are integrated into every aspect of the curriculum within a concentrated time frame, ranging from several days to a few weeks" (Kostelnik, 1996, p. 2). In the book *Themes Teachers Use* (Kostelnik, 1996) the authors describe what it means to use theme teaching in the classroom:

- Providing hands-on experience with real objects for children to examine and manipulate
- Creating activities in which children use all of their senses
- Building classroom activities around children's current interests
- Helping children acquire new knowledge and skills by building on what they already know and can do

- Providing activities and routines that address all aspects of children's development—cognitive, emotional, social, and physical
- Including a wide range of activities that address variations in children's learning styles and preferred modes of involvement
- Accommodating children's needs for movement and physical activity, social interaction, independence, and positive self-image
- Providing opportunities for children to use play to translate experience into understanding
- Respecting the individual differences, cultural backgrounds, and home experiences that children bring with them to the classroom
- Finding ways to involve members of children's families (Kostelnik, 1996, p. 2)

In an English as a second language (ESL) Training Manual (Burkart & Sheppard, n.d.), ESL teachers were given information about using themes in their teaching. Steps in the process included "(1) Selecting a Theme, (2) Brainstorming Associations, (3) Writing Questions, and (4) Developing Activities" (pp. 2–4). This manual also included information about adapting passages to help with comprehension. Some suggestions included:

(1) Write shorter sentences. (2) Simplify the vocabulary. (3) Simplify the grammar. (4) Rework the sentence entirely, if needed. (5) Add additional language for clarification. (6) Don't be afraid to repeat words, and (7) Use cohesive devices (e.g., then, such, first, however, it, also). (p. 7)

Teaching using themes lends itself to working with students who have different ability levels. It is also up to the teacher to "strive to create individual theme-related activities that cover a range of goals" for the student. (Kostlenik, 1996. p. 2).

After looking at the definition and basic steps for using a thematic approach in teaching, we decided this was the way we wanted to approach teaching literacy skills to our students. We were very adamant about using literature that was age appropriate, and this approach lent itself to using literature that was at the age level rather than the reading level of our students. Books could be adapted to student developmental levels, activities could be incorporated into daily schedules, and learning could be modified for individual learning needs. Now that the research had been done and steps in the thematic approach to teaching had been found, it was time to get to work and create the program that would be the most beneficial to our students.

PROGRAM OVERVIEW, PREMISE, AND GOAL

A school librarian is quoted as saying, "Encouraging people to develop real skills and transfer them to their lives is at the heart of literacy. Real literacy equals independence" (Pitcher & Mackey, 2004, p. 3). Independence should always be the goal of programs for students with special needs. A good literacy program is instrumental in developing this independence. Our program is based on a vision for excellence in literacy instruction for students with significant disabilities.

It is our philosophy that our students have the right to an exciting instructional program and that this program should be equal in quality to the general education program. As we sought to develop such a program, we examined our philosophy, established an overall goal, and listed the principles we consider basic in meeting this goal.

The program is based on the premise that students with moderate to severe disabilities can be successful in the acquisition of literacy skills. Our responsibility as teachers is to facilitate success.

The program goal is to assist students with moderate to severe disabilities with the acquisition of literacy skills.

PROGRAM PRINCIPLES

The following principles are at the core of this literacy program:

- The special needs and learning styles of the students should be kept at the forefront.
- When necessary, support and modifications should be provided.
- The program should be based on general education standards but should also emphasize functional skills.
- Materials and instruction should be age appropriate. Through the use of age-appropriate literature, our students can learn about and relate to adventures, families, faraway places, emotions, and the experiences of others while also gaining an understanding of their own lives.
- A team approach, which includes parents, should be utilized.
- General education opportunities should be provided.
- Planning should be based on a thematic or integrated approach. Through thematic instruction, our students make connections between life and the written word and among subjects such as science, reading, social studies, written expression, and math.

- A basic predictable structure for lesson presentation should be utilized throughout.
- A multisensory, multimedia, multimethod, and multilevel approach should be employed.
- Concrete materials and real-world experiences should be integral components. By constantly focusing on building background and language through media, real-world experiences, hands-on activities, dramatization, and real people, we are giving our students a rich world in which to develop literacy skills.
- Low- and high-tech assistive technology should be utilized to enhance learning and assure participation and success. Through the use of media and assistive technology, our students are developing both receptive and expressive language and are demonstrating comprehension and knowledge.

As stated earlier, students with significant disabilities have a right to exciting, well-planned, and appropriate instruction. The above-listed principles, when used as a foundation, provide the direction needed for the provision of quality instruction.

2 Establishing a Foundation for Planning

Teacher Objectives

- Consider special needs and learning styles of students in planning
- Use a team approach to ensure a multidisciplinary approach to planning
- Base planning on a thematic unit
- Use age-appropriate literature in the planning process
- Consider low- and high-tech assistive technology devices in planning

Planning literacy instruction for students with significant disabilities can be a daunting task. While general education teachers plan for a class of diverse students, they usually have a teacher's manual. In some states, general education teachers have supplemental manuals for teaching students with special needs. Special educators must plan for a group of students on many different levels with a variety of special needs. This is almost always done without a manual and with the need to find, develop, and adapt materials.

Special educators are required to teach based on standards while implementing individualized education plans (IEP) and meeting the needs of a diverse group of students. The teachers are given grade-level standards or extensions of standards and are often challenged by the task of translating standards into measurable, meaningful objectives for individual students. In addition, they must work to secure supports, build teams, and assure that resources are used at the best possible level.

Although the task of providing quality literacy instruction is not easy, it can be achieved. In order to accomplish this task, a teacher must transfer goals and standards into a plan for instruction. Even though all of the principles listed in Chapter 1 are important, the following five principles should be kept at the forefront of planning.

BASIC PLANNING PRINCIPLES

1. The special learning needs of all students should be considered.
2. A team approach should be utilized.
3. Planning should be based on a thematic or integrated approach.
4. Age-appropriate, meaningful literature materials and instruction should be utilized.
5. Technology should be used to support students with language and skills acquisition.

UNDERSTANDING THE STUDENTS

1. The special needs and learning styles of the students should be considered in all lesson planning.

Students placed in classrooms for persons with significant disabilities have a variety of strengths and needs. In order to be aware of the needs of students with moderate to severe disabilities, knowledge of their special learning characteristics is essential. Once this background knowledge is in place, one can then work to understand each student.

The students in our classrooms are intellectually disabled and are challenged by disabilities with varying etiology including Down syndrome, autism, cerebral palsy, traumatic brain injury, Rhett syndrome, and many other less frequently occurring syndromes such as Prader Willi, Dandy Walker, Angelman, and Cri Du Chat.

Learning Characteristics

Among the special learning challenges faced by students requiring limited to extensive levels of support are a slowed rate of learning, gross and fine motor skills difficulties, speech and language delays, sensory deficits, auditory processing problems, and difficulties with attention to task. Many are nonverbal.

According to Westling and Fox, (2004) students classified as having severe disabilities have difficulty with attention to stimuli, dimensions and cues, and observational and incidental learning. They also have difficulties with memory, skill synthesis, generalization, and self-regulation. Mesibov (n.d.) describes students with autism as having the following unique learning characteristics: organizational difficulties, distractibility, sequencing problems, inability to generalize, and uneven patterns of skills and deficits.

Alton (1998) describes the learning profile of individuals with Down syndrome as follows:

- Hypotonia
- Sensory deficits: hearing and vision
- Short-term auditory memory difficulties
- Speech and language problems
- Shorter concentration span
- Cognitive delay
- Difficulties with consolidation and retention of learning
- Generalization, thinking, and reasoning difficulties
- Strong visual awareness and visual learning skills
- Ability to use and learn sign, gesture, visual support, and the written word (p. 168)

Students with special needs face many difficulties. As a learner, each student is remarkably different. The more knowledgeable we are about the challenges faced by our students, the more effective and compassionate we will be as teachers. Along with the need for understanding the special challenges faced by students with special needs is the need for the provision of supports and modifications. It is not enough to know that a child has problems with attention to stimuli or difficulty with generalization or skill synthesis. This understanding must be followed by a plan for making the world of exciting and age-appropriate learning available and accessible. Challenges should always be viewed as a place to begin, not as a limitation

While the above information has touched briefly on a few of the special learning characteristics of groups of individuals with special needs, it does not begin to cover them in depth. That is a college course or a book unto itself. For this reason, it is highly recommended that you take the time to gain as much knowledge as possible about the known characteristics, needs, and challenges of your students.

TEAM APPROACH

2. A team approach should be utilized.

When developing a team for the delivery of thematic instruction for students with significant disabilities, it is important to realize that this teaching should be delivered and supported by individuals from many disciplines. Not only will the team have a need to deliver interdisciplinary (see glossary) services, but it will also be working to promote integrated learning. Students may need the support of a physical therapist, an occupational therapist, a speech pathologist, a counselor, a vision specialist, and family in addition to the expertise of a special education classroom staff.

In service-delivery models of the past, each specialist pulled students from the classroom and provided therapy or services in a separate one-on-one or small-group setting. Each discipline, while providing assistance for a specific need, was working in an isolated, disconnected environment. Skills were not easily transferred to the classroom or to life in the world. Gradually, a shift in the delivery of related services has occurred. Many therapists now support the students in the classroom environment, often working on goals written in collaboration with the teacher.

An exciting and natural next step is the building of a team in which all disciplines plan together for the education of the students. While a team is composed of individuals from many disciplines, the goal of collaborating to provide meaningful, exciting instruction is unifying. In the provision of services for students with significant disabilities, a team must not only plan for instruction but also work to provide access to education.

Our Team

A teamwork approach to our themes has been used, and it has served us well. In the beginning, our team was just the three of us: a speech pathologist and two teachers of separate classrooms for students with significant disabilities. As the news and excitement of what we were doing spread, the team grew. Some of the members of our team have been parents, paraprofessionals, a librarian, administrators, college professors, related services personnel, general education teachers, peer tutors, and teachers of classes such as music and art.

From the very beginning, the team met with our general education school librarian, Cheryl. As we began to consider teaching through age-appropriate literature, we explained our plan to Cheryl. She was enthusiastic and voluntarily compiled a list of potential middle-school literature that could be paired with video. She continued to be a wonderful part of the team by helping with technology issues and being on the lookout for new, interesting, and appropriate books for our students. She has also been helpful with teacher resources. In addition, she has been helpful in making sure we follow copyright law. She was always available to assist us in finding related supplemental materials, both fiction and nonfiction. Her expertise with school equipment such as liquid crystal display (LCD) projectors has likewise been invaluable.

After working during the summer to plan our units, we were excited when we returned to school to find that our teacher assistants became very involved in the units. They helped decorate the rooms and prepared materials for us. Later on, they came up with ideas for us to use and even taught some of the lessons. They have previewed movies for the books we were thinking about using and have let us know what they feel is appropriate. Having them on board and excited about what we were doing was an added benefit, and it also helped solidify the themes.

As we looked at the different things we wanted to do and accomplish, we expanded our team. First, we worked with our art teacher and explained our thematic approach. She used our theme ideas as the basis for her art lessons. In our "Dreams" theme using *Cinderella*, she had all the students bring in a shoe. There were tennis shoes, dress shoes, flip-flops, and a wonderful assortment of other types of shoes. The students then decorated those using paints, buttons, jewels, and glitter. They were beautiful decorations for our Cinderella Ball. During our "Determination" theme using *The Black Stallion*, she used the colors often depicted in African art on different textured rollers for the students to make posters representing that part of the world.

Our next step was to introduce more music into our themes. In our program, we have music once a week, and our music teacher covers four schools. Previously, the music taught was not related to what the students were currently learning. After we discussed it with her, the teacher was more than willing to work with our themes. During our "Outer Space" theme using *E.T.*, she exposed the children to *2001 Space Odyssey* and a song she found about space worms. During our "Friendship" theme using *Heidi*, she used music from *The Sound of Music* and had the students singing "Climb Every Mountain" and "The Lonely Goatherd."

Our guidance counselor has also become part of the team. In the past, she came into our classrooms once a week and read books or discussed social interactions and issues. Now, she reads a book or does a project based on our theme. When we read *The Secret Garden*, she helped the students build birdhouses. When we taught our "Friendship" theme, she brought in books and discussed what it meant to be a friend. She has also covered topics such as nonstereotypical gender roles for *The Whale Rider* and the dangers of running away from home for *My Side of the Mountain*.

The related service personnel provide essential support in helping our students access this curriculum. The speech/language pathologist is invaluable. Her expertise in language development is a good resource as we seek to choose vocabulary words to meet both goals in IEPs and extensions of the standard course of study. She creates communication boards and programs our communication devices. Her creativity in creating games such as bingo and hangman using theme vocabulary provides exciting multilevel opportunities for language skills practice. Her language sessions are conducted within our classrooms and even on community outings, providing real-life opportunities for interaction.

Our occupational therapist creates programs for skills reinforcement and helps facilitate access to computer programs and communication systems. Through her assistance, even the students with the most significant physical challenges are able to participate in comprehension and writing activities using technology. She works within our classroom making sure that each child's method of written expression is set up and ready for theme-related activities and interaction.

During a theme based on Asian culture, our physical therapist used martial arts to improve the physical fitness of our students. She accompanied us on a field trip to assist in facilitating participation in tae kwon do and yoga. She also works with us to assure that communication devices and materials used for written expression are accessible and properly positioned.

Our physical education teacher has been creative as well. Her use of PE time to help the students build on concepts being taught in our themes has been a pleasant means of reinforcement and generalization. When reading *The Jungle Book,* she adapted a bowling game into Coconut Bowling. In the theme "Outer Space," she set up a moonwalk by using a huge inflatable balloon.

We have also been very fortunate in that our program level directors and assistant directors have been very supportive of our efforts to teach age-appropriate literature. They have made money available for books and have encouraged us to raise the bar in education. Our Local Education Agency Special Services director and assistant director have also been very supportive and have encouraged our work.

In addition, the professors of Western Carolina University (WCU) have been a part of our team, by sharing their knowledge and expertise on age-appropriate, meaningful instruction. By placing interns and student teachers in our classrooms, they have guided future teachers into an understanding of teaching literacy skills through age-appropriate literature and thematic instruction. We have in turn shared our knowledge with groups of WCU graduate and undergraduate students.

These team members and their expertise and ideas have enriched our units and themes and have helped immerse the students in the literature. It has also given us a chance to meet and work with other teachers. Before, we often sent our students off to music, art, and guidance classes without always knowing what was going on in those classes. Now, we have an active team working within our classrooms, and our students benefit from the coordination of teaching.

Steps for Building a Team

- Begin by finding at least one teacher or related service provider with whom you share a philosophy and teaching style.
- Make tentative plans for your first thematic unit using the thematic unit planning sheet and the suggestions for choosing a book in Chapter 3 (perhaps the first theme could be one of the themes provided in this book).
- Make a list of potential additional team members. You may want to keep your team small in the beginning, until you are sure of the process.
- Schedule a planning meeting with the interested individuals to explain your ideas.
- Use the planning sheet to plan a thematic unit with the team (see the Sample Lesson Plans and Related Resources section for graphic organizer).
- Make plans for making materials and teaching the theme.

Some team members may be ad hoc members. For example, music, art and PE teachers may not be able to attend the planning meeting but may be very pleased to have the opportunity to relate instruction to the theme. For these individuals, e-mail or a brief discussion following their instructional time with your students will be adequate to explain the unit and possible ways for their participation.

Time for Team Planning

For many special educators, planning time is rare. Although this may seem like a time-intensive way of teaching, it is well worth your effort. In some ways, your work becomes less as you divide it among team members. It is recommended that you talk with your administrators about your plans to work together as a team. If at all possible, your administrators should provide a regularly scheduled time for team planning. It may be necessary to follow up large group planning sessions with a small core group to work out details such as field trips and how the instruction will be scheduled (see Chapter 3, "Building a Theme").

As we began our new program, we found the building of a team to be a wonderful, supportive experience, but we are aware that not all teams are built so easily. If you find difficulty in building a team, you may find the book *Consultation, Collaboration and Teamwork* (Dattmer, Dyck, & Thurston, 1999) to be beneficial.

THEMATIC APPROACH

3. Planning should be based on an integrated or thematic approach.

Thematic teaching has long been used by teachers in general education classrooms. Although it had its beginning in the general education classroom, this method of instruction serves students with moderate to severe disabilities well. In thematic instruction, a basic theme is chosen, and all other subjects are related to the theme. This makes it possible for students to understand materials and make connections rather than having isolated bits of information floating about without meaning or connection.

In the article "Thematic Instruction" (Northwest Regional Educational Laboratory, n.d.), it is stated, "Effective thematic instruction involves using a theme as 'conceptual glue' for learners, strengthening bonds to knowledge" (p. 1). Due to difficulty with synthesis and organization, the conceptual glue is critical. The interconnection of the subjects is enhanced, and information is grounded as students see how skills relate and are used in real-life situations.

There are many different ways to choose theme topics. Some teachers center teaching on a social studies or science concept. We choose to center instruction on a selection of age-appropriate literature from which we have chosen a theme.

Our Thematic Units

Our thematic unit "Mountain Heritage" (included in this book) was based on the book *Where the Lilies Bloom* by Vera and Bill Cleaver. By using *Where the Lilies Bloom* as a central focus for planning, we were able to teach geography concepts related to our Appalachian Mountains. In addition, we used this theme to teach the social studies concepts of family structures. We were able to teach about herbs that grow on the mountain slopes as well as those found in gardens. Through the teaching of mountain crafts, we were able to teach the science concept of melting (ice candles). The quilt activity provided an excellent occasion for teaching sequencing, guided reading, and geometric shapes. Making taffy provided a chance to teach reading and following written instructions. The trip to the farmer's market provided an opportunity to teach reading skills, language, purchasing skills, and counting. The related trip to the restaurant provided the opportunity for teaching language, manners, reading skills (menu), and money skills. Once the trip to the market was completed, the following days were spent reading and following directions for making soup, identifying vegetables, cooking, and measuring. Time was taught by discussing the length of time needed for the soup to cook and when it would be ready. One-to-one correspondence was taught as the table was set and silverware, bowls, and napkins were counted and put in place. Themes such as these also provide opportunities to teach functional skills (see Chapter 10).

A well-planned theme based on age-appropriate literature provides a wealth of opportunity for instruction. Not only does it open the door to the teaching of many skills and concepts, but each lesson is hooked into an overall net of understanding provided by the literature itself. We have a wonderful time weaving science, social studies, reading, art, writing, music, and math together into meaningful, well-integrated learning opportunities. The students likewise experience joy in learning. Thematic teaching is an outstanding avenue for providing appropriate instruction for our students.

THE USE OF AGE-APPROPRIATE LITERATURE

4. Materials and instruction should be age appropriate.

Many teachers of secondary-level students struggle with how to match the need for instruction with materials. As they enter middle school and even high school, numerous students with significant disabilities possess language arts skills at an emergent level. As described by Sulzby and Barnhart (1992), the skills they possess are not at the conventional literacy level but are at the skill levels preceding conventional literacy. Most books and reading programs designed for teaching beginning reading are intended for young children. While most students with severe to moderate disabilities are thrilled to be learning to read and will willingly work with such materials, they deserve much more.

For years, instruction for students with significant disabilities was based on developmental theory. The basis for this philosophy came from Jean Piaget, a biologist who studied the development of children and their levels of understanding. It was a common belief that individuals with significant disabilities were not psychologically mature enough for certain tasks and should prolong their studies at the lower levels until developmentally ready. Unfortunately, this theory prevented many individuals from being taught with materials that were fitting or proper for their age and has presented us with a significant void in the availability of appropriate resources.

The Three Pigs or *Brown Bear, Brown Bear, What Do You See?* are wonderful books and are fitting for preschool and kindergarten instruction. They can be a favorite to be read over and over by a parent at the student's bedtime, but adolescent learners should have the opportunity to move beyond these books.

In her book, *Transitions From Literature to Literacy*, Regie Routman (1988) states,

> It is important that children—particularly lower-achieving children who may not otherwise be exposed to the language of literature . . . be saturated with good books in the school environment. It has been my experience that vocabulary and multiple meanings of words are best learned and applied through the context of books. (p. 21)

Our students need exposure to the language of literature. This exposure should be offered through the richest materials available, since it is through these materials that language will continue to develop. It is apparent that *Little Red Riding Hood,* while teaching some language, cannot compete with the language opportunities available in books such as *Island of the Blue Dolphins* or *The Black Stallion.*

In addition to building language, age-appropriate literature provides an opportunity for students to compare the lives of others with their own. In books such as *Where the Lilies Bloom* or *Stone Fox,* young people face challenges and experience triumphs. Through the use of this type of literature, students are able to relate and gain insight into their own lives.

Routman (1988) states,

> Students relate easily to stories that deal with anger, sadness, jealousy, etc., and they have an opportunity to get in touch with their own emotions in a natural, nonthreatening manner. Readers meet characters who have traits like themselves, which makes them feel like an accepted part of the human race. (p. 21)

Many of our students, especially those with autism, have difficulty with understanding emotion. Through the characters in age-appropriate literature, they are able to see that others also face problems and feel sad, angry, or lonely.

Aidan Chambers (in Routman, 1988) states that "language is a condition of being human, literature is a birthright" (p. 20). Students with significant disabilities, like their general-education peers, should be given the opportunity to enjoy this inheritance. Through careful planning and scaffolding, it is possible to make the world of age-appropriate literature both available and accessible for students with special needs.

TECHNOLOGY

5. Low- and/or high-tech assistive technology should be utilized to enhance learning and assure success.

In her recent book, June Downing (2005) has this to say about literacy and communication: "Even if children with significant disabilities are given the opportunity to engage in literacy experiences, if they do not have the means to interact during these experiences, they cannot demonstrate what they know" (p. 10). That statement summarizes what should be the bottom line: Communication systems give students a way to interact, and teaching thematically through age-appropriate literature provides inspiration for interaction.

A considerable number of individuals in programs for students with significant disabilities are nonverbal. While there are a few students with verbal communication skills, most of these students have severe articulation problems. Without augmentative and alternative communication systems, there would be no way to know how students feel about the literature. Assessing comprehension would be greatly limited. Discussions would be inhibited.

There are many forms of communication devices on the market. In addition, there are programs available that make it possible to create simple communication systems. Because of the importance of assistive technology in our program, we have devoted the entirety of Chapter 5 to the subject. As you read the chapter, you will gain information that will assist you in both understanding the value of technology and working as a team to assure that your students have voices.

Table 2.1   Challenges/Implications and Solutions. This table lists challenges faced by individuals with significant disabilities, ways in which learning is impacted by these challenges, and how using the instructional techniques described in the following chapters helps facilitate learning.

Learning Characteristic	Impact on Learning	Benefits of Teaching the Literacy Beyond Picture Books Way
Organizational Difficulties	Students are unable to organize fragmented pieces of instruction into a meaningful whole	Teaching thematically provides a whole picture into which small pieces may be placed in a meaningful way
Distractibility	Students are easily distracted by environmental stimuli	The high interest level of meaningful literature and the strong use of visual information helps maintain focus
Sequencing Problems	Students have inability to place events of life and events of hypothetical situations in order	Through the use of literature, which is taught as a whole, then again in parts, the students gain a sense of story and of events in order
Difficulties With Consolidation and Retention of Learning (Skill Synthesis)	Students cannot on their own pull fragments of instruction into a meaningful whole and are likely to forget skills for which there is no meaningful attachment to life	Thematic instruction provides the glue for pulling together ideas and subject matter. Good age-appropriate literature helps our students understand their lives and relate to others. Reading skills are taught using a whole–to-a-part method; therefore the relationship between spoken and written word and symbol and sound become meaningful
Strong Visual Awareness and Visual Learning Skills (the Need for Visual Information)	A strength that can be used to greatly increase students' learning. If visual information is not provided, frustration is increased. Students have difficulty understanding, thus leading to inappropriate behaviors and decreased skill acquisition	By using videos, which help students understand literature, and by using special technology designed to provide visual cues, we capitalize on this strength/need
Auditory Processing Difficulties	Although the students are hearing normally, the brain does not easily process the information	A program that is strong in visual information, structured, and predictable is helpful
Speech/Language Delays	Students do not have the language needed to seek information, explore the world, and interact in learning situations	The use of technology, whether simple pictures, or complicated alternative communication devices, aids students in communicative interaction
Fine Motor Skills Difficulties	Students are unable to express themselves using traditional writing instruments	Technology, both low tech and high tech, aids in written expression

3 Building a Theme

Teacher Objectives

♦ Plan a theme

♦ Choose appropriate literature

♦ Brainstorm and use a graphic organizer to provide visual guidance

♦ Choose vocabulary

♦ Plan for community experiences

♦ Communicate with family or caregivers

When one considers the current requirements for educating students with significant disabilities, it is easy to become overwhelmed. Planning must include access to grade-level standards and meet individual goals. Thematic instruction provides an avenue for addressing these needs. *Building a theme* is a term that acknowledges a step-by-step process of understanding and implementing the basic steps in a thematic unit.

CHOOSING A THEME CONCEPT

Most often, students with significant disabilities have not experienced the world in the same way as their normally developing peers. Due to this, language development has been inhibited. The ability to understand and use language is vital for learning. Without this basic building block, other learning is inhibited. Bringing a good book to life and linking it to the world is an outstanding way to develop language. For this reason, our program is based on using age-appropriate literature as a unifying element in thematic instruction.

Due to the immense value of bringing a good book to life and linking it to the world, the choice of a concept for thematic instruction is secondary to the choice of a literature selection. The theme name is used only for the purpose of subject integration. It is chosen based on a concept supported by the literature and considered important to our students. Just because a theme may be called "Winter," for example, does not mean that six weeks of instruction will focus only on winter. Many instructional opportunities are inherent in fine literature and these can be woven together during theme development. The following pages will provide an explanation of how a theme is planned around a literature selection.

How to Plan a Theme

1. Preview possible books, and answer the following questions:
   a. Does the book offer an avenue for meeting course-of-study standards and teaching individual goals?
   b. Is the book age appropriate?
   c. Can it be paired with a DVD or video?
   d. Does your school have a license to show the video?
   e. Is the video approved by your administration, and if not, what papers do you need to complete to gain approval?
   h. What are your students like? Do they like animation? Do they like music?
   i. Are the majority of the students boys or girls?

2. Choose a book. After reviewing books with the above listed points in mind, it is time to choose a book (suggestions from other team members should be considered).

3. Meet with the team.
   a. Brainstorm ideas.
   b. Determine the length of the theme.

4. Use a Thematic Unit Planning Sheet and a Standard Course of Study Planning Sheet to plan.
   a. Agree on the focus of study and name the theme.
   b. Determine how standards from the course of study will be incorporated and how content areas will be integrated.

---

    c. Set goals related to language arts skills (example: choose a focus sound or sounds for phonemic awareness).

    d. Plan related activities such as field trips.

    e. Choose vocabulary.

5. Use the AssistiveTechnology Planning Sheet to work with specialists to plan for access and other special needs.

6. Finalize plans.

    a. Determine how individual goals, including functional goals, will be embedded.

    b. Make plans for assessment.

    c. Make community contacts and assure accessibility.

    d. Schedule events using a calendar.

    e. Talk with team members who may have missed the meeting, giving them a chance to connect to the theme.

    f. Write a letter to families, and include information such as a schedule of events and ways that their support will be needed.

CHOOSING A BOOK

As the research section (in Chapter 1) of this book verifies, very little has been published on choosing and adapting age-appropriate literature for students with significant disabilities. When choosing a main literature selection on which to base a theme, there are important criteria. These are questions to be considered:

- How will student goals be met?
- Will the students understand the content?
- Can the book be used to teach skills and concepts in the standard course of study?
- How can the literature be used to integrate science, social studies, math, and language arts?
- Have you read the book? It is not enough to know that it was a favorite of yours or your own children. It is important that you read it again through the eyes of a special educator to determine that the concepts and style of writing are appropriate for your students. Some books must be rejected. The rejected books may have a theme that is difficult to understand or they may involve violence or other disturbing material. Among the books we have rejected are *Tuck Everlasting* (because of the depth of understanding

it takes to understand the concept of eternal life) and *The Outsiders* (because of violence).

- Can it be paired with a video or DVD of the story? The use of a video to enhance understanding of the whole story is very important. In the past, teachers have depended on pictures in books to aid students with significant disabilities in understanding stories. These pictures are not present in middle-school literature. In addition, middle-school books are above the listening comprehension level of most students with severe disabilities. By using a video, the experiences necessary to build background and facilitate comprehension are provided. A perfect place to look for age-appropriate literature is the school library. It is best to choose literature that is well known. The classics are an excellent choice.

PLANNING

Brainstorming

The course of study or state standards should be kept in mind when determining the theme name or theme focus. Brainstorming with the standards in mind will help assure that the planning process is launched in a creative yet directed manner.

In brainstorming, all ideas are welcome. The acceptance of all thoughts establishes a safe working atmosphere, which promotes risk taking. Through the generation of many ideas, a rich theme will evolve.

As ideas are generated, they should be recorded on a large sheet of paper, visible to all participants. As is often the case, one individual's thoughts or ideas trigger the thoughts of someone else, those ideas trigger more thoughts, and this continues until a dynamic, creative theme emerges.

Once brainstorming has led to the generation of many wonderful ideas, the list should be edited to select the most suitable activities.

Graphic Organizer

In order to facilitate planning, a graphic organizer or a planning web should be used. It is through the use of this organizer that a team makes cross-curricular connections and plans exciting related activities.

As planning progresses, ideas for ways to integrate subjects and create learning opportunities will evolve. Organizing these thoughts on the graphic organizer will lead to an overall plan for instructional delivery.

Figure 3.1 Thematic Unit Planning Sheet (Graphic Organizer or Planning Web)

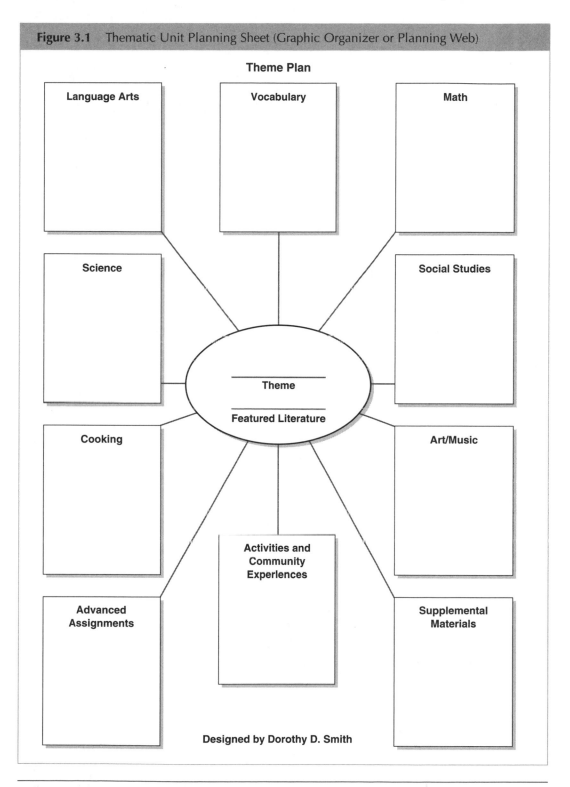

The graphic organizer provides the visual structure needed to assure that all core subjects are considered and included. The graphic organizer also provides a place to list opportunities for enriching activities and community experiences.

If more than two individuals are working on a theme, it is recommended that the team members have available a large graphic organizer. This may be made by drawing and laminating a chart-sized version of the planning web. By placing the web on the wall, and using dry erase markers, you can easily record and change information.

Choosing Vocabulary

Students with significant disabilities have considerable deficits in language. These deficits have been compounded due to the use of instructional programs with a narrow vocabulary. In this program, the vocabulary focus is wide. Part of planning for each new theme is choosing target content vocabulary words. Vocabulary is chosen by the team and is chosen for a variety of reasons.

Following is a list of reasons for choosing vocabulary:

- The word is important to the overall understanding of the literature. An example is the word *emerald* in *The Wizard of Oz*.
- A word is present in the literature, and teaching it in context will increase the likelihood that it will be learned.
- The need to increase the understanding of certain types of words— an example is the need to learn action words.
- Some students have a need to learn simple, concrete words.
- A right to know—it is not our place to decide that students with significant disabilities should only be taught some words or that they should not be taught certain words. This is the kind of thinking that has limited learning opportunities in years gone by. Students with special needs have the same right to acquire language as their normally developing peers. It is only through constant exposure and opportunity that this acquisition will occur.
- A word will increase an individual's conversational skills and make it possible to communicate with peers, family, and other members of the community.

We have designed the vocabulary for each theme to be multilevel. We strive to include words from different levels in order to meet the needs of most of our students. Some students are more able to understand concrete words such as *bat* or *snail*, while others may be able to comprehend less concrete words such as *destiny*, *tradition*, or *confident*.

Within a classroom of students with significant disabilities, there are often students who are readers, able to read the printed word. Some students are only able to read symbols. It is important to design the word cards to meet the needs of both the readers of text and the readers of symbols. This may be done by including both a symbol and its corresponding word on each card. Within each of the lesson plans at the back of this book (see the Sample Lesson Plans and Related Resources section) are sample vocabulary cards, which can be copied for classroom use and also serve as a model for you to create cards for your own reading selections.

FINALIZING PLANS

Individual Goals

As was mentioned at the beginning of this chapter, it is important to select literature that will allow for teaching course-of-study standards and individual goals. Once the theme planning has taken place with goals in mind, it is time to plan how individual goals will be embedded and monitored. Careful planning at this stage of theme development will increase the likelihood that connected learning will take place (as compared to the drilling of skills in isolation).

Planning for Assessment

If a thematic unit is planned with individual goals and the standard course of study in mind, instructional time will provide opportunities for assessment and data collection. Listing the target goals on the weekly lesson planning sheet will alert all classroom staff to a need to collect data on individual goals. Other team members, such as the speech pathologist and occupational therapist, may also find the instructional time related to the thematic unit appropriate for data collection. Chapter 9 is devoted to assessment. Within the chapter are ideas for using instructional time for assessment.

Planning for Community Experiences

Outings into the community are among the most powerful learning opportunities available to students with special needs. For this reason, planning is important. This planning should occur as soon as the development of a theme begins. The list of potential field trips generated during the brainstorming phase of planning should be evaluated and narrowed. Among the questions to ask when finalizing field trip plans are the following:

- What can be gained?
- How does the potential outing relate to the theme?

- Is the destination handicapped accessible?
- Is the cost reasonable?
- Is the activity available during the instructional day?

Planning is completed by checking with managers of potential sites and with administrators to arrange dates, times, transportation, and special accommodations.

Packing for Community Experiences

When packing for a trip, we are always sure to include communication systems, cameras, and plastic zip top bags. The students can use the cameras for capturing memories and fill the bags with souvenirs. The photographs and souvenirs are placed in the students' writing boxes and used as writing starters. The communication systems are a must if students are to build language through community experiences.

Many of our students have significant physical needs and require different types of equipment throughout the day. It is beneficial to make a packing list for each student. List medicines, special foods, tube-feeding equipment, pullups and diapers, extra plastic bags, and cleaning supplies. Materials for behavior plans (such as reinforcers and checklists) should also be included. Each classroom should have a separate book bag that goes on field trips. Having a packing list helps keeps things organized and helps staff remember important items.

SCHEDULING EVENTS

Once the team has completed the steps in planning the instruction and activities for a theme, it is time to schedule events. A planning calendar is needed. By placing the events on the calendar, you develop a good visual guide, allowing the team to place instruction and related activities into place in a way that makes learning connected and sequential. For example, if the book *The Wizard of Oz* is being read, it makes sense to have the trip to see all types of roads at the beginning of the unit and as close to reading about the yellow brick road as possible.

PARENT COMMUNICATION

Most often, families want to be and are involved in the education of their children. Students with significant disabilities sometimes have difficulty talking with the family about the school day. For this reason, it is the responsibility of the special educator to keep families informed.

When exciting learning is taking place, families want to share in the excitement and, when possible, provide reinforcement for the learning at home. A parent letter providing a day-by-day listing of activities is an effective way to introduce the units. In addition, the letter provides notice when there will be a cost or a need for assistance with materials.

Letters to families are also used to explain theme-related homework. This homework might involve projects, or it may be just vocabulary review tips. Keeping families involved assures good response and lots of help with the projects and homework.

Below is an example of a letter to families for the thematic unit "Winter" featuring *Stone Fox*. Similar letters are written for all thematic units.

Dear Parents,

We have now started reading *Stone Fox*. It is a story about a courageous boy on a potato farm who takes care of his grandfather and races with his beloved dog. Our theme this time is "Winter," and we have some interesting and fun activities planned. Many of them involve eating! Please notice dates that have a * by them because you will receive more information about them as the dates approach.

As always, please let us know if you have any comments or suggestions.

Jill and Josh

February 20	Begin *Stone Fox*
	Watch *Stone Fox* movie
February 21	Winter Haikus
	Discovery Education *streaming* video on winter
February 22	Read Chapter 1
	Retell (journal)
*February 25	Read Chapter 2
	Retell (journal)
	Iditarod art
	Pick arctic animal for presentation
February 27	Grow Borax snowflakes (science experiment)
	Winter walk and poem
February 28	Mrs. Jan's (our counselor) group—worrying
February 29	Read Chapter 3
	Introduce vocabulary
	Different types of races
*March 3	Introduce the Iditarod race
	Choose dog for race

(Continued)

(Continued)

March 5	Read Chapter 4 Retell Vocabulary Potato facts French fry day
*March 6	Field trip Ryan's Steak House Krispy Kreme Doughnuts
March 7	Read *Owl Moon* Make snow flake art Watch the movie *Snow Dogs*
March 10	Read Chapter 5 Retell Vocabulary
*March 11	Send in presentations
March 12	Read Chapter 6 Retell Vocabulary Potato print art
March 13	Counselor's group—money
March 14	Native American names Watch the movie *Brother Bear*
March 17	Stages of water Make snow cream in a bag
*March 19 & 20	Presentations
March 21–March 30	Spring break
March 31	Read Chapter 7 Retell Vocabulary
April 2	Read Chapter 8 Retell Vocabulary Potato chip cookies/potato pancakes
April 4	The Dog Man (dog that does tricks) Watch *Surf's Up*

April 7	Read Chapter 9 Retell Vocabulary
April 9	Read Chapter 10 Retell Vocabulary
*April 10	Field trip to Happy Tails
April 11	Watch *Stone Fox* Theme Celebration

Feb. 25—Refer to the additional information about the arctic animal your child chose.

March 3—The Iditarod dog sled race in Alaska begins on March 1. Since the book is about a dog race, each classroom will be choosing a dog to follow in the race. We will be looking at the Web site daily and tracking our particular dog.

March 6—We will be going to Ryan's Steak House to eat at the potato bar (in the story, the boy lives on a potato farm), then go to Krispy Kreme for doughnuts and hot chocolate—a real winter treat! Please send in $8 for this trip.

March 19 and 20—Please come to the student presentations. We will let you know when your child will be presenting.

April 10—Please send in $7 for lunch.

ADDITIONAL PLANNING AIDS

In addition to the graphic organizer (Thematic Unit Planning Sheet), we have found other planning aids to be helpful. These include a planning sheet for connecting the theme to standards, and an assistive-technology planning sheet.

The following planning sheets are available in Sample Lesson Plans and Related Resources.

- Thematic Unit Planning Sheet (a graphic organizer or map for the basic planning of a theme)
- Standard Course of Study Planning Sheet (a form for connecting the standard course of study to the theme)
- Assistive Technology Planning Sheet (a form for planning for individual technology needs)

Each thematic unit included in this book contains a completed Thematic Unit Planning Sheet (Theme Plan). The activities listed are only suggestions.

BUILDING A THEME: A CHECKLIST

- ❐ Meet with your team
- ❐ Choose a book (make sure that you have read the book)
- ❐ Brainstorm
- ❐ Plan ways to link to the standard course of study
- ❐ Choose vocabulary
- ❐ Complete the Thematic Unit Planning Sheet
- ❐ Make field trip contacts
- ❐ Schedule activities and literacy instruction using a calendar
- ❐ Complete family letter

Setting the Stage

Teacher Objectives

♦ Structure the classroom to facilitate instruction, including the arrangement of the physical environment and scheduling

♦ Create visuals to add excitement and cues for learning in the classroom

♦ Create hands-on materials to increase sensory input and help make connections between the theme and an activity

♦ Prepare assistive technology devices to assure that students who are nonverbal are able to participate

♦ Develop classroom materials that support instruction

A s with any play or production, setting the stage is a very important part of the theme process. Getting prepared to teach and having everything in place creates a calm and organized space in which to instruct. It is always helpful when the students feel the teacher knows what is going on in the classroom. A pattern of instruction yields familiarity and a sense of rhythm. This is especially helpful for students with autism or those who need a more orderly approach to instruction. This is not to say that spontaneity cannot happen during instruction. In fact, setting an organized stage facilitates spontaneity because the basics are taken care of so creativity in students and teachers can occur without disrupting the instructional process.

PROVIDING STRUCTURE

In classrooms for students with significant disabilities, chaos is not only possible but also probable if appropriate structure is not provided. Students are assisted in understanding the classroom world through the provision of structure. When students are given an idea of what to expect, the learning curve increases, and energy and attention are directed toward educational activities.

Structure is provided in many ways throughout the day, including arrangement of the physical environment and schedules. Visual information is made available to help with understanding, and predictability is enhanced through routines. It is through this kind of support that our students are able to attend to instruction at a higher level and for longer periods of time. Without such structure, large-group instruction, such as theme time, would likely be unsuccessful.

Among the supports provided to students during theme time are seating arrangements designed to provide for maximum staff support and a routine in which core instructional activities remain the same for each thematic instructional opportunity.

STRUCTURING THE CLASSROOM ENVIRONMENT

The physical structure of the classroom is a critical part of structuring the theme. Just as structuring an entire theme is important, the day-to-day seating of students is very important. Students who need help with communication devices or need extra assistance should be paired with a teacher assistant or a nondisabled peer tutor. Those who may need to leave frequently (students who walk to manage agitation, those with bathroom issues, etc.) need to be seated nearest a door. Students who are sleepy because of medicine or sleep apnea need to be near the front so the teachers can encourage them to stay awake. Students who agitate each other should be placed apart. Students who are functioning at a higher level can be paired with students who are functioning at a lower level. Students in our class help point out letters, vocabulary words, and characters to those who do not know them or have difficulty with fine motor movements.

STRUCTURING ACTIVITIES

It is important to keep a similar routine for each large-group theme lesson. When core activities—such as viewing a video, reading a book, retelling a chapter, and working with content vocabulary—are taught in the same order during all thematic lessons, the students know what to expect. The addition or substitution of different activities then becomes simply a matter of informing the students of the change.

Not all theme-related lessons can be structured the same way. In other words, while a "normal" theme day may involve vocabulary study, reading, and retelling, there will and should be days that are different. For these days, schedules of activities that occur should be available in all forms needed for your students. This may include objects, symbols, or words.

Certain theme-related activities such as arts and crafts require stronger structure than others. When teaching a group activity designed to produce an expected product, it is important to have a demonstration model ready. It is also important to work together as a group and progress through the steps in an orderly manner.

Printing step-by-step instructions on a large chart is one way of facilitating success. You can use objects, symbols, words, or a combination of the three. This not only provides structure and aid to success but also creates an excellent opportunity for teaching word identification and the sequencing of events through guided reading.

SCHEDULING

In order to accomplish all that we should throughout the day and in theme time, we must leave little to chance. Following is a sample of how our day is scheduled in order to provide opportunities for both individual instruction and group instruction opportunities such as theme time.

Individual Student Schedules

Once a good overall classroom schedule is in place, the needs of students, such as those who have autism, can be met through individual schedules. For students with significant disabilities, and especially those with autism, routine and predictability are essential. Schedules reduce stress, thus allowing the students to focus on the learning activities. Individual schedules should be at the reading level of the student, such as written schedules for readers, symbol or picture schedules for symbol readers, and objects for nonreaders.

For some students, it is imperative that they know not only what is happening across the day but also what will occur within each large block of time such as theme time. For those students, an activity-specific schedule that lists events that will occur within the block of time is helpful.

Scheduling Breaks

For some students, a successful experience during theme time is dependent on the scheduling of a break. For these students, an opportunity for movement or quiet is built into the theme routine. This should be listed on the student's individual schedule. The break may be in the form of a walk with an assistant, time away from the group on a computer, or time in a separate quiet room.

Table 4.1   Weekly Schedule

	Monday	Tuesday	Wednesday	Thursday	Friday
8:00 a.m.	Arrival Bathroom Choice centers	Arrival Bathroom Choice centers	Arrival Bathroom Choice centers	Arrival Bathroom Choice centers	Arrival Bathroom Choice centers
8:45	Group	Group	Group	Group	Group
9:15	Self-selected reading/reading to students (books selected by students)	Self-selected reading/reading to students (books selected by students)	Theme	Self-selected reading/reading to students (books selected by students)	Self-selected reading/reading to students (books selected by students)
9:30	Writing minilesson	Writing minilesson	Theme	Writing minilesson	Writing minilesson
9:45	Students write	Students write	Theme	Students write	Students write
10:00	Theme	Assigned centers/one-on-one instruction	Theme	Assigned centers/one-on-one instruction	Theme
10:45	Theme	Guided reading; book or activity	Prepare for lunch	Guided reading; book or activity	Theme
11:00	Theme	Guided reading	Lunch	Guided reading	Theme
11:30	Prepare for lunch	Prepare for lunch	Depart for swimming at the gym	Prepare for lunch	Prepare for lunch
11:45	Lunch	Lunch	Dressing for swimming	Lunch	Lunch
12:00 p.m.	Lunch	Lunch	Swimming or gym	Lunch	Lunch
12:30	Physical activity	Physical activity	Swimming or gym	Physical activity	Physical activity
1:00	Math	Math	Dressing	Math	Math
1:15	Math	Math	Return to campus	Math	Math
1:30	Working with words: word wall and making words	Working with words: word wall and making words	Working with words: word wall and making words	Working with words: word wall and making words	Working with words: word wall and making words
2:00	Home/ school journals (This is one journal)	Home/ school journals	Home/ school journals	Home/ school journals	Home/ school journals
2:30	Prepare for departure	Prepare for departure	Prepare for departure	Prepare for departure	Prepare for departure
2:40	Departure	Departure	Departure	Departure	Departure

Providing structure in the form of schedules, routine, and an organized physical environment is important to success. Our theme time and related activities are exciting and filled with fun, but joy in learning does not happen accidentally. Successful teaching is at least in part the result of careful structuring.

ENHANCEMENT OF THE CLASSROOM ENVIRONMENT

When the school year begins, the classroom is a bare and utilitarian space. It is up to the teacher to put touches in the classroom to make it a warm and inviting place conducive to learning. Bulletin boards add a great deal to the anticipation and excitement the students have with theme time. When the students first come to school at the beginning of the school year, much of the classroom is decorated in a theme.

Photo 4.1　　A bulletin board designed to build excitement as a theme is launched

The classroom setup is an essential part of the units. In our classrooms, there is an area for "theme time." In this area are the vocabulary words for the unit. Each word is on a 3 × 11-inch card that has the word along with the Boardmaker symbol. The words are placed alphabetically on the board or wall.

Characters from the book often adorn the walls. Tom, Huck, Cinderella, the Black Stallion, and E.T. have been on our walls. The old-fashioned opaque projector comes in handy! When the students do the

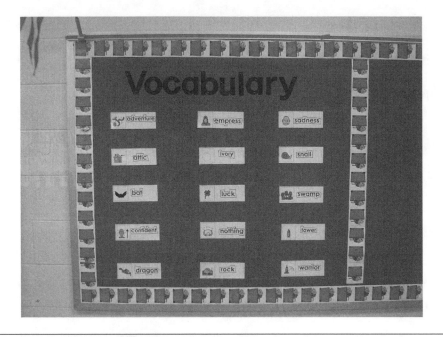

Photo 4.2   Vocabulary display in theme area

theme-related art, it goes up on the walls or bulletin boards. When the students bring in their posters or other items for the presentations, these also go on the walls. By the end of the unit, most of the classroom walls are covered with unit-related materials. It is colorful with a lot of variety and is composed mostly of the work the students have done. The students have access to the words and the characters of the literature we are reading, and it helps them through the learning process.

One year, we started with the theme "Courage" using *The Wizard of Oz*. The bulletin board outside one of the classrooms had scenes from the movie and the title, "We're off to see the Wizard!" Inside the room, two-foot-high characters in the movie were on the wall, and the background was the yellow brick road.

Vocabulary words with symbols from the unit were in the theme/ group area, and communication devices were already set up with words from the unit. As the year progressed, student art went up on the bulletin board and walls. The students enjoyed seeing things related to the theme they had produced. Often, their art spilled out onto the walls of the halls. We have had "Poppy Art" and Munchkins from *The Wizard of Oz* and The Nothing from *The Neverending Story*.

Students could see their art as they walked back and forth through the school. They have enjoyed hearing comments from other teachers and students about their work. Accompanying the art is a phrase or quote from the book. This helps provide a text-rich environment, and individuals not involved in the theme can relate to and understand the art.

Photo 4.3   A mural from *The Wizard of Oz*

Retrieved July 15, 2005, from http://thewizardofoz.warnerbros.com/cmp/cpic20.htm

Visual enrichment has become a very important and highly anticipated part of the themes. Initially, the visual information helps keep students engaged during the theme process. As their work is added to the room, it helps show the students their work is valued and is an addition to the learning process.

PROVIDING MATERIALS FOR HANDS-ON LEARNING

In the "Research" section of Chapter 1, it was discussed that a basic premise of using a thematic approach to teaching is to allow students many hands-on materials to explore with their senses. After you begin a theme and expose the students to the prepared visuals, it is important for the students to make a connection between the visual and auditory information they are taking in to real-life applications. Hands-on activities help students make this connection. For each theme, hands-on activities and lesson plans are made.

For *Island of the Blue Dolphins*, a teacher made dresses out of leather/suede material (which looked like animal skin) for two large, dark-skinned dolls that looked like Karana.

These dolls were available to the students to look at and hold during the theme. In *Little House on the Prairie,* students gathered sticks from the woods nearby and constructed a log cabin.

In *The Wizard of Oz,* students made roads out of their choice of materials, including dirt, rock, bricks, and sandpaper (representing a paved road). The activity was also a writing opportunity when the students completed the sentence, "I want my _____ (insert *paved, dirt, brick,* etc.) road to take me to _____." Students inserted pictures or wrote where they wanted their road to take them. (Instructions for this activity are available in the Resources included in this book.)

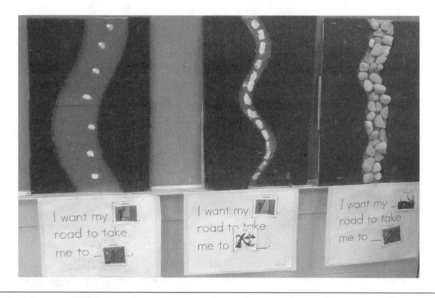

Photo 4.4   Student work showing both artwork and written-expression opportunities

One of the vocabulary words for *The Wizard of Oz* was *emerald.* Some of our students had heard this word before, but we wanted to make sure they knew it was a substance found in nature and not just the color of the city in the story. For a hands-on activity, we brought in many different types of stones, rocks, and items made of different types of those materials.

An activity using birthstones was used, and a large picture of each of the birthstones of the year with the month in large letters under the picture was created. The picture and the stone (or similar stones such as zirconium rather than a real diamond!) for each month were shown. *Emerald* was highlighted, and the students were reminded that it was a vocabulary word. The students had been given a piece of paper shaped like a stone with their name and birth month on it. They put the stone under the name of the month they were born, and it became a graphing exercise. The teachers and teacher assistants were also involved in the activity.

Photo 4.5 A theme-related math lesson in which students graphed birth months

Hands-on activities and materials help make things real to the students. An image of Karana or a log cabin becomes tangible. An idea of what a stone or color may look like becomes something a person can hold and feel. These connections are important as the students try to relate the things they are hearing and seeing to things that happen in their everyday lives.

PREPARING TECHNOLOGY

Preparing the technology is a time-consuming but important part of the preparation for teaching a theme. It is essential that each student have an opportunity to ask a question or to share an answer or opinion. When provided with appropriate tools, it is amazing the information that the students who are nonverbal can share with the group. At the beginning of the school year, it is a good idea to complete an Assistive Technology Planning Sheet found in the Sample Lesson Plans and Related Resources section to thoroughly assess the communication needs of the students.

In their CD *Out and About: AAC in the Community,* Wagner, Musselwhite, and Odom (2003) developed strategies for supporting a student's optimum use of their augmentative and alternative communication (AAC) device by understanding the roles of the communication facilitator and communication partner. In thematic instruction, the communication facilitator and partner have important roles.

The communication facilitator is the person who makes sure the device and user are ready. This person is often the speech/language pathologist, but may also be the teacher or assistant. Assuring that the device and user are ready includes

- Designing and programming overlays/pages with appropriate vocabulary, ensuring that the device is charged and ready, and helping the child get to the correct overlay or page prior to the activity or interaction

- Making sure the user is ready for the interaction by teaching applicable concepts, allowing for practice of the vocabulary, and teaching strategies for rate enhancement if applicable
- Making sure the environment is ready by providing training for the communication partner if needed, putting hints for the partner on the device, and helping the user find a position where he or she can see the partner and access the device
- Cueing appropriate device use during the interaction by providing the least level of prompts needed for success

The communication partner is the person who is interacting with the device user. It is important that the communication partner be informed of his or her role in advance and assisted in understanding this role. This person may be a peer tutor, an assistant, a teacher, or other individual in the student's life. The role of the communication partner includes

- Showing respect for the user by using age-appropriate language and tone of voice as well as expecting a response
- Asking open-ended questions
- Providing frequent pauses to allow the user to have a turn to talk
- Providing opportunities for turn-taking
- Accepting multiple modalities of communication
- Allowing the facilitator to cue device use rather than specifically asking the child to use the device (Wagner, Musslewhite, & Odom, 2005)

The speech/language pathologist usually sets up communication devices, but this may also be the responsibility of other team members. Some of the students have powerful communication devices such as the Dynavox, but for the most part, the Zygo Macaws, Black Hawks, and low-tech communication notebooks are sufficient. Each vocabulary word with its corresponding Boardmaker symbol is put on the devices. The symbols are omitted, and words only are used for students who are readers. Pictures of the characters of the particular theme are put on the devices so a student can answer *who* questions. Included on the devices is also a page with common answers that can be used for the theme or for other activities. This page has phrases such as, *I like it, I don't like it, This is fun, I know the answer, yes, no,* and other phrases used in communication.

In order for students to listen to the story at a less difficult listening comprehension level, software, such as BuildAbility, is used to create a condensed version of the story. Peer tutors can also assist in creating illustrations and text using this program.

IntelliTools programs such as Classroom Suite are another type of technology that is very useful. Vocabulary words and comprehension questions can be created through the use of this program. Students can use the program to read the question, push a button, or use a mouse to answer the question, then check to see if it is correct. This is a helpful program for assessing reading comprehension skills of students with significant disabilities.

Because preparing the technology can be time consuming, we have found it beneficial to take turns doing different tasks. If one team member, be it speech pathologist, occupational therapist, or teacher, writes a BuildAbility story, the other can write questions using Classroom Suite. If one person creates the vocabulary words, another can program the devices.

It is important to have as many ways for a student to communicate as possible. Let every student have a voice, and you will be as surprised and as thrilled as we were to hear what your students have to say.

For additional information on assistive technology, see Chapter 5.

OTHER CLASSROOM MATERIALS

Large Chart Tablets: We use these extensively. When a chapter of the book is read and we have a lesson on retelling, teachers take turns writing what the students say when they are asked about the story. It is large enough for everyone to see, and it gives us a chance to discuss certain letters we may be targeting. The chart tablets also give organization to the story, and it is easy to go back and forth throughout the theme and use the retellings as a large, easily seen book, written at a simpler level.

Three-Legged Easel With Large White Board: So students can see everything that is written, either an easel with a white board or a chalkboard is used to provide a firm support behind the chart tablet. The chart tablet is attached to the easel by clamps. This gives a sturdy area for writing, and it is also portable and easily taken down and put away after theme time.

Markers: Heavy-duty permanent-ink markers in different colors (chiseled edges make the neatest letters) are used. Students are given the choice of color for writing the retelling, poetry list, or other writing lesson for the day. Purple is the favorite color so far!

Highlighters and Highlighting Tape: During *The Wizard of Oz*, the letter *W* was a focus because of the vocabulary words used, such as *witch, wizard,* and *wicked*. During retelling, if a *W* was used, students were asked to come up and highlight the letter. This was also helpful when targeting different letters during phonics time. Highlighting helps reinforce the new letter or one being repeated during theme time. During journaling, if the student uses a vocabulary word in a sentence, highlighting the word is another way to review the vocabulary and show how it can be used in the story. Highlighting tape has also been discovered. This is similar to scotch tape but comes in many different highlighting colors. Since the tape is about as big as the letters we write during journaling, the tape is a precise way of identifying particular letters. The students enjoy putting the tape on the letters, and the letters seem to "pop out" and become more easily identifiable.

Name Boxes: Every student and staff name is put on a small card, then laminated and placed in a box with a lid (such as a wet wipes box). This comes in handy throughout the day during retelling and asking for responses from nonverbal students, deciding who goes first to answer a question or identify a vocabulary word, or to determine order in telling a favorite part of the story. This helps students pay better attention because they are not sure who will be chosen next. It helps give those students who do not volunteer information as easily as others a chance to participate. It is also an important way to teach the skill of name recognition by just pulling the name out of the box and holding it up. The students watch and read the names. The teacher then reinforces the efforts by calling the student by name while holding up the card. The students also enjoy it when a staff member's name is drawn to see if they are able to give the correct answer.

These name cards are also an easy data-collection system. As each student is asked a specific goal question, the name card can be placed in one of two containers, *correct* and *incorrect*. Data can later be recorded on data sheets.

SETTING THE STAGE: A CHECKLIST

☐ Choose an area of the classroom to dedicate to theme instruction
☐ Prepare and display bulletin boards, murals, and other visuals
☐ Prepare three sets of vocabulary cards for the classroom and one for each student
☐ Set up a display area for vocabulary, and display one set of words in alphabetical order
☐ Prepare and display hands-on materials (dolls dressed as characters from the literature, related science materials, books and magazines with related topics, games, related music CDs, etc.)
☐ Prepare pages for communication devices and for low-tech communication systems
☐ Prepare a theme folder for each student (we use these folders for sending home vocabulary words and copies of chapter retellings for students to share with their families)
☐ Prepare any games you plan to use, such as bingo
☐ Gather materials such as charts for retelling, an easel, markers, and highlighters, and place them in the theme area

5 Providing Access Through Assistive Technology

Teacher Objectives

- Understand the definition and use of assistive technology
- Understand the accessibility features of operating systems
- Access technology vendors
- Understand low- and high-tech devices used in thematic units

ASSISTIVE TECHNOLOGY

Technology is leading to an exciting new world of educational opportunities for individuals with disabilities. The field of assistive technology is ever emerging and expanding. As the field of technology grows, so do opportunities for individuals with special needs.

Through the use of assistive technology, individuals who once were unable to speak can now tell tales. Individuals who were unable to write can now write volumes. For individuals with significant disabilities, technology is providing access to learning once thought to be an impossible dream.

The term *assistive* or *adaptive technology* commonly refers to "products, devices or equipment, whether acquired commercially, modified or customized, that are used to maintain, increase or improve the functional capabilities of individuals with disabilities"(Assistive Technology Act of 2004).

Assistive technology may be considered appropriate when it does any or all of the following things:

- Provides access for participation in activities that otherwise would be closed to the individual
- Assists in expressive language
- Increases endurance or ability to persevere and complete tasks that otherwise are too laborious to be attempted on a routine basis
- Allows greater access to information
- Supports normal social interactions with peers and adults
- Helps individuals achieve greater independence in performing daily living tasks

For the purpose of this book, we will be dealing with assistive technology tools needed to increase a student's literacy skills in the areas of oral and written expressive language.

Augmentative Communication

Every student in school needs some method of communication in order to interact with others and learn from social contact. Students who are nonverbal or whose speech is not intelligible enough to communicate effectively may benefit from using some type of augmentative or alternative communication (AAC) device. Communication devices include such features as objects, symbol systems, picture communication boards and wallets, dynamic display communication devices, such as a Dynavox or Vanguard, eye-gaze systems using pictures or words, recorded-speech devices that offer a single message or series of messages, and voiced word processing found in software, such as IntelliTools Classroom Suite or Kurzweil Educational Systems.

Writing Aids

Writing is an easily understood method of expressing preferences and opinions. Writing tools found in a typical classroom include pencils, markers, letter stamps, cookie cutters and modeling clay, magnetic letters, white boards, and writing or drawing toys. Many times, students have difficulty getting their thoughts on paper because of physical limitations affecting the writing process. Pencil grips, magnetic word banks, eye-gaze systems, and dictation to a scribe are low-tech ways to address these issues. Computers or word processing devices offer another output method. Adaptations for computers include touch screens, alternative and adapted keyboards, key guards, head pointers, and switches. Software accommodations include text to speech, word prediction, spell check, scanning features, screen magnification, and voice-recognition systems.

Photo 5.1   An IntelliTools keyboard used for written expression

Dr. Gretchen Hanser at the Center for Literacy and Disabilities Studies in Chapel Hill, North Carolina, has developed a series of Alternative Pencils to use with students who have significant disabilities. Information concerning how to find complete instructions for making these "pencils" is in the References section (see Erickson & Hanser, 2004). These alternative pencils include:

- Alphabet Flip Chart
- Braille Alphabet Flip Chart
- Braille Intellikeys Overlay
- Color-Coded Eye-Gaze Frame

All writing materials should be readily available in the writing area of the classroom. Teachers should model writing using a variety of materials. As students begin using the writing tools, the teacher should engage in parallel writing activities to expand the student's understanding of how to use the tools.

Digital Books

It is important for every student to be able to access books read to the students or written by the class. Book pages can be stored on a computer via a scanner or document cameras such as ELMO or Ken-a-vision. These pages can be projected on a white board with a data projector, making them large enough so students who have visual impairments can see them. SmartBoards or a mimio Interactive Board can turn the white board into an interactive board for increased opportunities for multisensory learning. Software such as PowerPoint, IntelliTools Classroom Suite, My Own Bookshelf, BuildAbility from Attainment Co., and Hyperstudio by Roger Wagner are useful tools for helping the students create their own digital books. These books can also be printed, expanding the collection on the classroom bookshelves. The Internet provides tutorials for many of these programs as well as templates for simple storybooks.

Accessibility Features

Microsoft and Apple Corporations have offered increased accessibility features built into their operating systems. Starting with Windows XP, these features are found in the START menu > ACCESSORIES > ACCESSIBILITY. In the Mac operating systems, look in APPLICATIONS > SYSTEM PREFERENCES > UNIVERSAL ACCESS. These features include

- Changing the font size on the entire system
- Switching to a lower screen resolution to increase the size of items on the screen
- Sticky keys—if the student finds it difficult to hold down several keys at once (e.g., CTL+ALT+DELETE) this feature will let you hit one key at a time
- Bounce keys—if the student accidentally hits a key more than once, this feature ignores repeated keystrokes
- Mouse keys—if the student has trouble using a mouse, he or she could use the numeric keys instead
- Mouse cursor—to choose the size and color of the mouse cursor
- Mouse speed—changes the speed of the mouse pointer, if the student has difficulty positioning the mouse pointer to select items

Table 5.1 lists some vendors offering assistive technology devices:

Table 5.1 Technology Vendors

Vendor	Products	Web Address
AbleNet, Inc 2808 Fairview Avenue N Roseville, MN 55113 800-322-0956	Big Mack Step by Step Super Talker MeVille to WeVille Curriculum many switch options (formerly from Tash, Inc.)	www.ablenetinc.com
AMDI, Inc. 200 Frank Road Hicksville, NY 11801 888-353-AMDI	Tech/Touch Tech/Talk Tech/Scan	www.amdi.net
Assistive Technology, Inc. 333 Elm Street Dedham, MA 02026 800-793-9227	Mercury II MiniMerc Link Lightwriter	www.assistivetech.com
Attainment Co. Inc. PO Box 930160 Verona, WI 53593 800-327-4269	GoTalk, BuildAbility My Own Bookshelf Math and money materials	www.atttainmentcompany .com
Don Johnston Inc. 6799 W. Commerce Drive Volo, IL 60073 800-999-4660	Reading and writing materials; products are organized by skill levels and include both access and learning interventions	www.donjohnston.com
DynaVox Technologies 2100 Wharton Street Suite 400 Pittsburgh, PA 15203 888-697-7332	Series5 Mighty Mo Dynamo Dynawrite	www.dynavoxtech.com
ELMO Company LTD. 1478 Old County Road Plainview, NY 11803 800-947-ELMO	ELMO visual presenters and document cameras	www.elmousa.com

Table 5.1 (Continued)

Vendor	Products	Web Address
Enabling Devices 385 Warburton Avenue Hastings-on-Hudson, NY 10706 800-832-8697	Cheap Talk: seven-level communicator Many switches, toys, and devices	www.enabling devices.com
Key Technologies 411 South King Street Morganton, NC 28655 888-433-5303	Vendor for all major manufacturers; it also provides training on products sold	www.gokeytech.com
IntelliTools 1720 Corporate Circle Petaluma, CA 94954 800-899-6687	Classroom Suite, Intellikeys, many software programs supporting literacy and math; check out the Activity Exchange on the Web site	www.intellitools.com
Ken-A-Vision, Inc. 5615 Raytown Road Kansas City, MO 6413 800-627-1953	Projection equipment and document cameras	www.ken-a-vision.com
Mayer-Johnson, LLC PO Box 1579 Solana Beach, CA 92075 800-588-4548	Boardmaker Picture Symbols, Speaking Dynamically Pro, basic augmentative communication devices, and many teacher resources	www.mayer-johnson.com
mimio-Interactive A Newell Rubbermaid Company 25 First Street Suite 301 Cambridge, MA 02141 877-696-4646	mimio-Interactive offers an interactive white-board solution	www.mimio.com
Prentke Romich 1022 Heyl Road Wooster, OH 44691 800-262-1984	Vanguard Vantage Pathfinder Chat Box	www.prentrom.com

Vendor	Products	Web Address
RJ Cooper 27601 Forbes Road Suite 39 Laguna Niguel, CA 92677 800-752-6673	Special education software and hardware products	www.rjcooper.com
Slater Software 351 Badger Lane Guffey, CO 80820 877-306-6968	PixWriter, Picture It	www.slatersoftware.com www.tashinc.com

TECHNOLOGY IN OUR PROGRAM

Communication

Our classrooms are built around opportunities to communicate in alternative ways. Students are encouraged to comment with phrases such as "You look like you have something to say," "What do you think about that?" or "Your turn!" It is essential that each student have a voice and a chance to share.

Low-Tech Communication

In addition to mid- and high-tech systems, low-tech communication systems are constantly in the hands of our students. We make available our low-tech communication systems to all students, even those with the more powerful devices.

Low-Tech Communication/Language Book

Over the years, we have developed a low-tech communication system, which is in the form of a notebook. These notebooks are language books that aid spoken communication as well as written expression. The notebooks are made with three-ring binders. D-ring binders are best because the cover can easily be folded back to make the book lie flat on a student's lap.

The primary purpose of the notebooks is to provide an always-available dictionary and voice for the words our students have learned or are learning. Each notebook has a core vocabulary composed of words often used in daily conversation and classroom instruction. These words are in such typical categories as people, transportation, outdoors, places, and foods.

Each system also includes theme-specific vocabulary. The theme-specific vocabulary remains in the notebooks along with the core vocabulary after the completion of the theme. The next vocabulary page is simply added when a new theme is begun. Our students often refer to previous theme pages in subsequent themes. The words become a part of their individual vocabularies, and just as we speak from our past experiences and pull from our own vocabulary repertoire, so do they. If vocabulary words are removed, students tend to forget the content. If we take away the theme-specific vocabulary after the theme is complete, we remove their voices for those words.

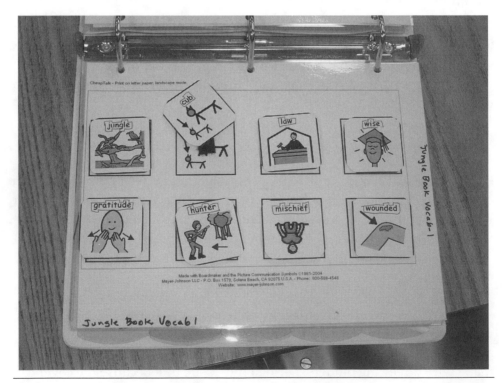

Photo 5.2   Adapted communication notebook providing continuous access to vocabulary words

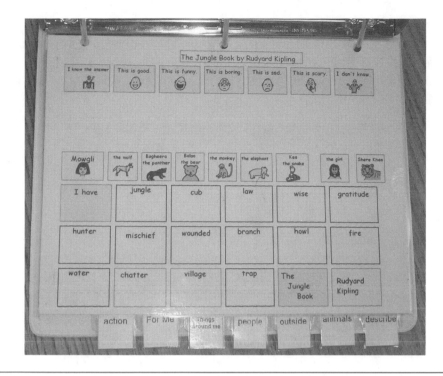

The Jungle Book by Rudyard Kipling

| I know the answer | This is good. | This is funny. | This is boring. | This is sad. | This is scary. | I don't know. |

| Mowgli | the wolf | Bagheera the panther | Baloo the bear | the monkey | the elephant | Kaa the snake | the girl | Shere Khan |

I have	jungle	cub	law	wise	gratitude
hunter	mischief	wounded	branch	howl	fire
water	chatter	village	trap	The Jungle Book	Rudyard Kipling

| action | For Me | things around me | people | outside | animals | describe |

Photo 5.3   Communication notebook with words only for a more advanced student

In addition to leaving the theme pages in place for future reference, we use the theme vocabulary to teach language lessons. This is done by helping the students glue an extra copy of each word in the appropriate category in their communication notebooks. These lessons are one more step in helping students understand language. In subsequent lessons, a student can search for a certain vocabulary word either on the original theme page or in the appropriate category.

By using the notebooks throughout the day, and especially in our highly motivating theme time, communication is maximized. The students not only learn to communicate during theme time, but they are motivated to communicate throughout the day as well. These books were designed to move with the students as they progress through the grades.

To assist with written expression, each notebook is equipped with a copy of a QWERTY keyboard, and a piece of laminated, white card stock attached (by Velcro) to the outside. Inside each notebook is a pencil pouch with a dry-erase marker and a small piece of flannel to be used as an eraser. When teaching a thematic lesson, we often have the students close the notebooks and use the outside for writing. We also use the keyboard for the teaching of prewriting skills and for the assessment of sound-symbol relationships. This notebook is an excellent tool for assessing the written expression and phonics skills of individuals.

As teachers of students with special needs, we have been given the awesome responsibility of making communicative interaction possible for all learners. It is our job to assure that all learners have a voice and even their own individual pencil. Although this is a complex challenge, the result is well worth the effort.

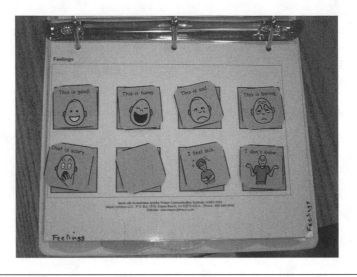

Photo 5.4   An adapted communication page designed to assist with accessibility needs

We use technology in many forms. Among these are digital cameras, LCD projectors, computers, expanded keyboards, word processing programs, DVD players, VCRs, the Internet, and high- and low-tech communication systems. Throughout the following chapters, you will find numerous ideas for incorporating technology into instruction for students with disabilities.

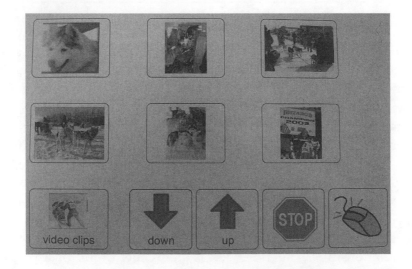

Photo 5.5   An Intellikeys overlay for the Internet when learning about the Iditarod during a theme based on *Stone Fox*

6 Instructional Delivery

Once the planning is completed and the stage is set, it is time to begin instruction. While many teachers may jump ahead to this part, it is very important to have organization behind the instruction.

THEME INTRODUCTION

There are many exciting ways to introduce a theme. In the whole-language approach often used by general-education teachers, the study of a book is begun by exploring the cover, sharing the title, and telling about the author. The introduction is continued with a picture walk through the book. Once the picture walk is completed, an opportunity for predicting the events of the book is provided. This basic plan for introduction is sound and should be used and enhanced with adaptations and variations.

Because the introduction of a new book is a wonderful opportunity to build excitement when launching a theme, it should be presented with considerable drama or fanfare. There are many ways to introduce books. Playing games or bringing a character in costume into the classroom promotes enthusiasm and anticipation. One example is the visit of an astronaut at the launch of our "Space" theme. Another example is the launching of the theme "Growing Things," using *The Secret Garden.* A big poster was made. Doors were cut into the poster, and clues in the form of pictures and/or words were placed behind the doors. Student names were pulled from the name box. When a student's name was pulled, the student was allowed to open a door, name the clue, and make a guess about the theme. We continued this process until all of the doors were opened. Although the students never guessed the name of the theme or book, they had a lot of fun and were fully engaged by the time we brought the book out of hiding.

Conveying excitement about the new literature and all of the possibilities that it holds will set the stage for wonderful learning. As is the case of elementary education instruction, the presentation of new literature should begin by sharing the book cover. At this point, the name of the author and the title are shared, and students are given an opportunity to predict what the book is about. For this lesson, as is always the case, students should have access to communication systems. The low-tech notebooks may be a good choice for most individuals due to the availability of previously learned vocabulary.

The next step in the introduction of the literature is the viewing of the video in its entirety. During the first showing of the video, it is best not to interrupt the video. The students need to become immersed in the plot and enjoy the experience. This gives the learners an understanding of the story as a whole, providing the background necessary for comprehension. For some students, especially the ones who are new to this type of instruction, the viewing of a movie in its entirety is difficult. It is to be hoped that you will choose a first theme that is very engaging, such as ones based on *The Jungle Book* or *The Wizard of Oz.* If you still have difficulty sustaining the attention of some learners, those learners should be given a scheduled break during the movie (see the sections on structure in Chapter 4, "Setting the Stage"). You will find, as we did, that students' attention levels increase as you do more themes.

In addition to the viewing of the movie, other activities may be used to build background. Maps are a good method for showing students the geographical setting of the story. A data projector and an Internet connection might be used to introduce students to the locale. Characters of the video may be introduced by way of the movie trailer on the Internet.

As you work to plan themes, you will discover that there are many creative ways to introduce a new theme. However you choose to lead the students into a new theme, lead them with joy and excitement. It will be contagious, and a good time will be had by all.

INTRODUCING VOCABULARY

If one is to interact with others and discuss a good story, then one must have a voice and words. For this reason, it is important to introduce the theme vocabulary at the beginning of a theme. By the time a theme is introduced, the vocabulary cards should be finished, and the words should be in the communication devices and notebooks.

After the initial introduction of the literature and the first showing of the movie, it is time to present the new vocabulary. Once again, this can be a time of excitement and anticipation. Anticipation can be built by keeping the words hidden and by making a production of the introduction.

In Chapter 4, "Setting the Stage," we explained that the word cards are made with both symbols and words. It is suggested that you make three copies of the words for each classroom and one copy for each student; see the lesson plans in the Sample Lesson Plans and Related Resources section of this book for sample vocabulary cards related to different reading selections. Two of the classroom sets are kept whole (words and symbols together). One of the sets is displayed in the theme area (see Chapter 4 for an example). One set is cut apart (words are separated from the pictures). These sets are used for instruction.

When the vocabulary words are introduced, it is best to use the entire word card, including the symbol. Through this process, the students who are readers are provided with print, while the emergent readers are provided with a print model and a way to understand and discuss the literature. The words are kept a secret from the students until this special introduction day. On the day that the words are introduced, they are brought out of hiding and introduced one at a time. In our theme time we take turns presenting a new word. We do so by keeping the word covered and then saying, "This word means . . ." or "This word is something that . . ." and then showing the word and picture to the group as we say it aloud.

A good practice when introducing the vocabulary for the first time is to have individual communication systems and theme notebooks in the hands of the learners. These communication devices and notebooks should already be programmed with the new words. This provides an opportunity for the learners to become familiar with the location of the words on the theme page. During this lesson, staff and peer tutors should be intermingled in the seating arrangement and should assist students with locating the words on the devices.

SHARING THE LITERATURE CHAPTER BY CHAPTER

After the initial showing of the movie, it is time to begin teaching the literature chapter by chapter. On some days, a teacher may focus on reading a chapter of the literature, while on other days the focus may be on a related activity.

It is suggested that the reading of a literature selection be conducted in a fashion similar to reading a chapter book, one chapter at a time. When two teachers are working together, this reading should be presented in a turn-taking fashion. The alternating of two voices makes the reading more engaging. Be aware that this reading is from an age-appropriate book. This assures the students are being exposed to the flow of language and vocabulary at a higher level. The value in this is similar to the value of reading a book to a very young child. Even though the child may not know all of the words, first you read, and then you explain using the pictures. The literature selection may be above the listening comprehension level of your learners, but this gap will be filled in by the use of the video and the reading of the retellings and adapted books. It will also be filled in as you stop the video and explain and relate it to the literature and the vocabulary words. Review the previous chapter before going on to a new chapter. Following this, the new chapter is introduced.

As each new chapter is begun, it is good practice to guide students in predicting what will happen in the chapter. Once again, the communication notebooks become a powerful tool. The students have not only the theme-related vocabulary available but also the vocabulary of other themes and the general vocabulary. Out of all of these words, students are provided what is needed to make connections and predictions.

Once the reading of a chapter is completed, it is time to show the related section of the movie. During this viewing, the remote control is used to stop the movie for the purpose of assisting in comprehension and connecting vocabulary to content. Much can be taught as the movie is stopped to point out geographical features, talk about a sequence of events, name characters, or make connections between the story and vocabulary.

RETELLING

Retelling is a process used to assess comprehension of a previously read book or chapter of literature. In this process, students recall the sequence of events and tell the story of the book or chapter in their own words. When students are asked to use their own words and write their own retelling, the teacher is able to assess many skills, including comprehension, sequencing of events, comprehension of sentence structure, spelling skills, and grammar.

Retelling, with a teacher leading the process, is an excellent opportunity to model written expression. Due to deficits in language skills, students with disabilities benefit greatly from this kind of group lesson. The language is spoken and then written. The students are then able to understand the connection between spoken and written language.

The retelling process is a perfect time for the assessment of individual language-arts goals in a naturally occurring setting (see Chapter 8 for data sheet examples). Through questioning designed for students at many different levels, a variety of skills may be assessed. Individual goals should have been a part of planning, and related data sheets should be available for recording progress.

When a retelling begins, students should be seated in a group facing the teachers. Staff and peer tutors should be intermingled with the students and ready to help facilitate interaction and prompt and record data. Materials should be ready. Essential materials are a large chart tablet on an easel. A large white board makes a good solid surface to stabilize the chart tablet when placed on the easel behind the tablet. In addition, chisel point permanent markers will be needed.

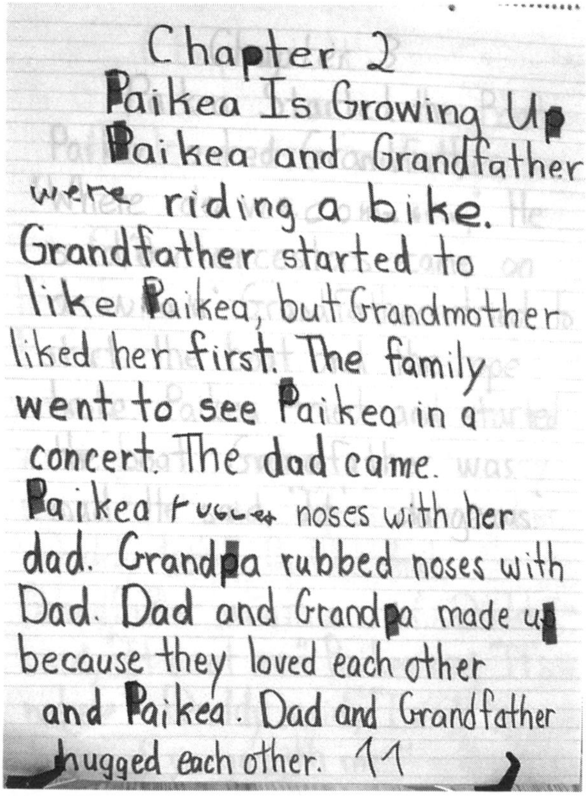

Chapter 2
Paikea Is Growing Up
Paikea and Grandfather were riding a bike. Grandfather started to like Paikea, but Grandmother liked her first. The family went to see Paikea in a concert. The dad came. Paikea rubbed noses with her dad. Grandpa rubbed noses with Dad. Dad and Grandpa made up because they loved each other and Paikea. Dad and Grandfather hugged each other.

Photo 6.1   A chart showing a recorded retelling math skills, highlighting of the consonant P, and sharing the pen

The retelling process begins with the brainstorming of a chapter title and continues with the learners retelling the happenings of the chapter in their own words. Students who use communication devices should have their systems in hand so that they too may volunteer information to be recorded on the large chart paper. The retelling is teacher led, but students should be involved in the writing process. Student involvement includes such activities as recalling events of the story, spelling words, or providing initial and final consonants and word endings.

All students should have available a laminated copy of the QWERTY keyboard. This provides the students who are minimally verbal and nonverbal a way to participate in the spelling process. Students should be encouraged to use the copies of the keyboards to point to letters if they are unable to verbalize suggestions for spelling (see Photo 6.2).

The teacher may also use the keyboards as a way to prompt. If a student is asked what sound is heard at the beginning or end of a word, the keyboard may be used to prompt the student to success. This is done by giving visual choices on the keyboard. For example, the teacher may be recording a sentence about the beach from the literature selection *The Black Stallion*. The teacher may tell the students that she needs help in spelling the word *beach*. Some students may be able to answer the question immediately. Other students may need to have additional support and be prompted to success by being asked, "Does beach begin with a *B* or an *R*?". To help clarify the question and to help the students make sound-symbol connections, a staff member may point to the two choices on the keyboard. The student then chooses a letter, and if the student is nonverbal, the staff person states the chosen sound to the class. The use of the keyboard in this fashion helps familiarize the students with a standard or adapted QWERTY keyboard and leads to a smooth transfer to independent writing.

If a student uses a communication device such as a Dynavox, the keyboard of the device may be used in a similar fashion. The voice output feature will allow the student to verbalize the choice, rather than having to depend on a staff person.

Not all students have the motor skills needed to select between two choices on a copy of a keyboard. For these students, the letters of the alphabet are printed on cards and Velcro is attached to the back of each card. When a staff person presents choices to the student, the letter choices may be easily narrowed and offered in a less cluttered and more easily accessible manner.

Photo 6.2   Communication notebook showing QWERTY keyboard

Example: Retelling of Chapter 3, "Willy Drives the Herd"

The following passage is an actual retelling of a chapter in *Stone Fox*. There are many types of questions and statements that can help students think about what is going on in the chapter and the movie. It is a very interactive process between the teacher, teacher assistants, and the students. Following this representation of Chapter 3, "Willy Drives the Herd," you will find the actual teacher questioning that led the students through the retelling process.

> ### Retelling of Chapter 3 of *Stone Fox*, "Willy Drives the Herd"
>
> Willy took some of the herd to sell for money to pay the taxes and buy hay. It was a cold winter. Willy heard howling. The wolves were trying to eat the herd. Willy shot at them with a gun.
>
> When Willy got to the stockyard, he found out he would only get $5 for each cow. That would only be enough money for hay. Willy was worried.

As you read the following questions, it is important that you refer back to the completed retelling above to see the progression of the writing. Student responses to the questions are not listed but may be observed in the actual retelling. For example, in question one, the teacher said, "We have done Chapters 1 and 2. What chapter is next?" If you refer back to the retelling shown above, you will see that the response was "Chapter 3." Once this was written, the teacher then led the students through the process of determining a good title, and the title was then written by the teacher.

Retelling Questions for Chapter 3, "Willy Drives the Herd"

- We have done Chapter 1 and Chapter 2. Denny, which chapter is next?
- Does anyone have a good idea for a chapter title?
- What was the main thing that happened in this chapter?
- Look at your communication page. Which character is in this chapter the most?
- Look at your characters in this book. Wesley, what letter does *Willy* start with?
- Did you notice that *Willy* and *Wesley* start with the same letter?
- Danny, what letter makes the "HHHH" sound? Jordan, can you show me the sign for the letter *H*?
- Let's go back to the first part of this chapter. Why did Willy have to sell some of the cows? Use your vocabulary words to help with a sentence.
- Rikki, what is the first letter in *taxes*? Jessa, what letter makes the "SSSS" sound at the end of the word?
- Think about the weather. Do you remember in the movie when there was snow and the lake was frozen? How does it feel outside in that type of weather?
- What happened next? Christian said, "Willy heard howling." What animal makes the howling sound? Everyone make a howling sound.
- Sebastian, we know that Willy hears howling. Come up and act out what happens next.
- Jaime, spell *the*.
- Chris, did the wolves want to play with Searchlight or eat the cows?
- Kevin, spell the word *gun*.
- We know that Willy took the herd to the stockyard. What happened when he got there?
- What symbol do I need in front of the 5 to make it look like money? Elizabeth, come and draw it.
- Alicia, I know that a cow is your favorite animal. Come up and write the word on the chart.
- Kelli, does Willy have enough money for everything?
- What happens when something is bothering you and you can't get it off your mind? How do you feel? Jeff, look at your vocabulary page, and give me a sentence about how Willy might feel.

You did a great job with the retelling. I am going to read it first, and then I want you to read along with me.

- Now that we have read the retelling, let's find a letter. Look at this last sentence. What letter do you see a lot?
- When I call out your name, come to the board and highlight (with highlighting tape) the letter *W* or a vocabulary word.
- Let's count how many Ws there were in this chapter. Let's see how many vocabulary words there are.

As you can see, for an eight-sentence retelling, there is a lot of questioning that is possible. More beginning and ending letters could be asked, and more words could also be spelled. Spelling questions about frequent words such as *and*, *to*, and *the* could also be asked.

Sharing the Pen

As teachers are recording the retelling of the chapter on the chart tablet, students should be invited to *share the pen.* This is a term used when students are provided opportunities to write words or letters on the chart. This strategy can be very individualized. If a child is at an emergent level, writing an A or an L may be a gratifying accomplishment. For some students, the independent spelling of complete words is possible. Sharing the pen is an excellent way to build skills necessary for independent writing. It is also a good way to assess the language skills of individuals during group instruction.

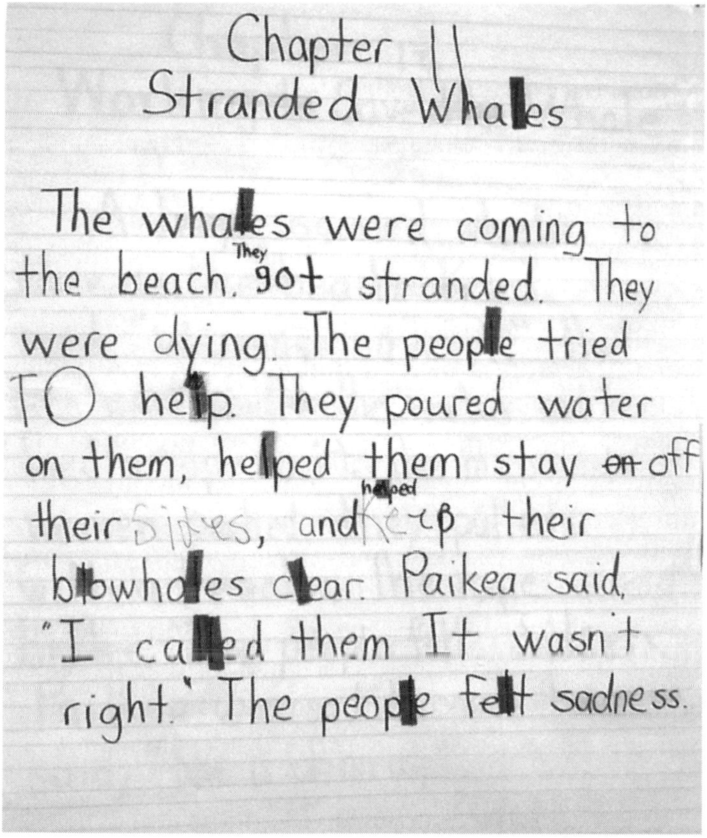

Photo 6.3   Retelling of Chapter 11 in *The Whale Rider.* Note "sharing the pen" for "got," "to," "keep," and "sides" and highlighting letters

Using the Word Wall

As a retelling is taking place, we often refer to our word wall for assistance in spelling. This word wall is not the vocabulary display but rather a display of frequently used words. It is used to show already-taught sight words such as *and, is, the, was* and *you.* The words are placed on the wall under the corresponding alphabet letter as they are taught throughout the year. Each word under each letter should be mounted on a different-colored background. When retelling, the teacher may ask for assistance in spelling a high-frequency word such as *their*. She may suggest that the students look at the word wall and find the word. Hints may be given, such as, "It is the green word under the letter T."

Once the word is found, the teacher models it by writing the word into the retelling entry. The students will learn to refer to the word wall and will subsequently incorporate this strategy into their daily independent writing. It is also wise to have individual folder-size copies of the word wall available. This provides students with a closer model and allows staff to provide a higher level of prompting by pointing to words.

Using the Retelling Entry for Instruction

After the retelling of the chapter is completed, the recorded retelling should be used as a guided reading lesson. When using the chart for this purpose, it is read aloud by the teachers and then by the students as a group. In addition, individual students should be given the opportunity to read the chart independently.

The retelling entry may also used for other instructional purposes. A good tool for this lesson is often a highlighter or highlighter tape. The teacher should set a goal and ask the students to assist by highlighting the answers. This is a perfect time to teach sound-symbol relationships in a naturally occurring situation. Students may be led to find words that have certain sounds at their beginnings or endings. A student with more advanced skills may be asked to find all compound words or to find all words with an *ed* or *ing* ending.

For vocabulary instruction, students may be asked to help identify all of the current content vocabulary words included in the text. Skills at a higher level may be taught by asking students to find a word with a certain meaning.

The retelling is also a good way to teach components of text. For example, students may be asked to search for the title or to point out a sentence or a paragraph. The teacher is teaching the top-to-bottom and left-to-right concepts needed for good print processing. An opportunity is provided to teach punctuation and capitalization and, last but not least, reading. The reading is at the listening comprehension level of the students and provides an opportunity for hearing and reading the text at a more easily understood level.

The instructional possibilities for using a chapter of literature, as it is retold, are many. The retelling provides opportunities for instruction for a group of students with a wide variety of needs, and as the teachers prompt to success, each child will be a winner. As the teacher encourages and praises each student's successes, all students feel safe and willing to share knowledge.

TEACHING VOCABULARY

Vocabulary lessons should be interspersed throughout the theme. These lessons are fun for the students and can be used at the end of the theme time when a little movement and interaction are beneficial. Below, you will find the steps of typical vocabulary lessons. These lessons are multilevel. Some students are learning that pictures can be used for language, and some are learning to read words. Some students are learning the meanings of small, concrete words, and some are learning the meanings of more difficult words.

Teacher Materials

- Name box (described in Chapter 4, "Setting the Stage")
- A set of vocabulary words displayed on the wall in the theme area
- A set of vocabulary cards with words and symbols still connected
- A set of vocabulary cards with the words and symbols cut apart

Student Materials and Supports

- Each student should have available a low-tech communication notebook with a vocabulary (theme) page or a communication system preprogrammed with the vocabulary
- Staff and peer tutors should be seated beside students who may need assistance

Learning New Words

When the words are new, the lesson is simply to teach the students to recognize the words. This may be done by holding up a word card (sound and symbol together) and saying, "This is the word _____. Can you find the word _____?" Staff should give the students wait time, and then prompt as needed until all students have located the words on their theme pages. Continue until all words have been taught. This lesson should be taught again on subsequent days until the students are able to locate the words.

Teaching Word-Symbol Recognition

Using the set of vocabulary words that have been cut apart into symbols and words, staff should pass the cards out to the students. Students who are emergent readers should be given a symbol card and a simple word. Students who are conventional readers should be given the more challenging words.

The teacher uses the word cards that are not cut apart. Without showing the word-symbol card, the teacher asks, "Who has the picture of _____?" Either independently or with staff assistance, a student indicates that he or she has the word. The student is then prompted to say, "I have _____," using either a communication device or words. The teacher then says, "Who has the word _____?" The student with the word then says, "I have _____." Prompting as needed is used after the

(Continued)

(Continued)

students are given ample wait time. This prompting is usually done by a staff person. After this process, the teacher collects the word and the symbol and displays them together side by side or shows her copy of the word-symbol card. At this point, the teacher may use the word in a sentence, talk about how the word is used in the book, or give a definition of the word. Continue until all vocabulary words have been taught.

Teaching Word Meanings

The process for this lesson is the same as lesson for teaching word recognition, but in this lesson the teacher says things such as "Who has the word that means _____," or "I am thinking of a word that means _____." Other sentences could be used, such as, "In the book, Willy felt _____ because his grandfather had no money. Who has the word that tells how Willy felt?"

Photo 6.4   Students looking for words during vocabulary lesson

Vocabulary instruction can take many forms. Ideally, the words are taught not only in lessons such as the ones described above but also throughout the teaching of the theme. Opportunities are always present when watching the video or reading chapter by chapter to stop the video and show the word and symbol. For example, when watching the scene with the flying monkeys and the Wicked Witch in *The Wizard of Oz*, the teacher might stop the video and talk about courage. A generalization opportunity for teaching the word *money* when reading *Stone Fox* could be

Photo 6.5   Student identifying vocabulary word

the trip to Krispy Kreme or Ryan's Steak House, when the students are using money to pay for food.

GUIDED READING

Cunningham and Allington (2007) give the definition of *guided reading* as guiding "some students—whether a whole group, small group, or individual—through an activity designed to help them apply their word identification and comprehension strategies" (p. 180). This definition is descriptive and inclusive of the key components needed to teach through guided reading.

Guided reading is often used to instruct individuals and small groups, but when teaching thematic units, it is often used for instructing a larger group of students. This instruction may occur for the purpose of teaching word-identification skills, increasing oral-reading fluency, and developing comprehension skills. Among the materials used for guided reading instruction are the following:

- Sets of informational books by companies such as Newbridge
- The journals *Time for Kids* and *National Geographic Explorer!*
- Recipes on large charts
- Words from songs featured in theme-related movies printed on large charts

- Daily chapter retellings written on large charts
- Web sites on related science, geography, or social studies topics (displayed using a data projector)
- Poetry printed on large charts
- Student-created books
- Theme-related, peer-tutor-created books
- Theme-related nonfiction and fiction selections

Photo 6.6 Making our own constitution led to opportunities for teaching literacy skills when reading *The Jungle Book*

Classrooms of students with significant disabilities are usually multilevel; therefore, each guided-reading selection is used for multiple purposes. Although special education teachers are constantly teaching many skills to many levels through each guided-reading selection, some materials lend themselves well to a particular focus skill.

- When using a recipe written on a large chart, the focus may be on reading for information and sequencing of events.
- When accessing information on other lands through a data projector and the Internet, the focus may be on map reading.
- When using a large chart to teach the words to songs such as tunes from *The Wizard of Oz*, rhyming words may be taught. In addition, the words may be used as a transitional text for students who need wording that is repetitious.

- When using a chart for the retelling of a literature selection, the focus may be on comprehension.
- When using sets of informational books such as the Newbridge selections, the focus may be on reading for information.
- When using additional theme-related fiction selections, the focus may be on comprehension strategies, such as identification of main characters, main ideas, and sequence of events.

Teaching through the use of age-appropriate literature and a thematic approach provides many ways to teach skills through guided reading. The students are given the foundation and the conceptual glue through the thematic approach. Guided reading helps provide the building blocks for the development of language arts skills.

BUILDING LANGUAGE

As you examine our Thematic Unit Planning Sheet, you may become immediately aware of the front-and-center position held by vocabulary. It is no accident that vocabulary holds this prominent place. One cannot overemphasize the importance of vocabulary in receptive and expressive language as well as in reading and writing.

For many students with significant disabilities, participation in normal language-building experiences has been limited. For this reason, they do not have meanings for a lot of words and are playing catch-up. It is important to constantly build vocabulary through both targeted words, such as vocabulary words, and in a rich, experience-filled environment.

Background-building experiences are designed to help provide connections between words and the world. As stated earlier, themes are based on age-appropriate literature. Although it is wonderful to offer this literature to students with disabilities, the books may be above the listening-comprehension level of the individuals.

In order to assist students with comprehension of middle-school literature, it is important to build background. When real-world experiences are not possible, one should recall the old cliché, "A picture is worth a thousand words." Media can be used to help the students form mental images, thus assisting in the understanding of the literature.

For each thematic unit, background-building experiences begin with the viewing of a movie based on the chosen literature. Watching the movie helps provide the foundation needed for building understanding.

In addition to viewing a movie based on the chosen literature, media can be used to provide experiences in other ways. Web sites or trailers of the movie are invaluable for introducing the students to characters. Virtual trips into the land in which the movie is set provide opportunities to teach social studies-, science-, and geography-related vocabulary. The vocabulary associated with animals, plants, peoples, and terrain is just a click away. All of the above and more can be achieved through the use of a data projector and a large screen.

COMMUNITY EXPERIENCES

Well-planned and well-taught trips into the community rank at the top of language-building experiences. Because experiences build language, it is important that at least one of the trips occur at the beginning of the unit. Taking a camera along and snapping pictures for use in reading and writing helps to maximize the benefits of the experience.

When possible, inexpensive digital cameras should be provided for student use and should be taken on field trips. Once the students have returned to campus, the photos may be used for individual journaling or to make classroom books about the experience.

Photo 6.7   A winter outing to Krispy Kreme

PREDICTABLE CHART WRITING

An excellent method for teaching writing using the experiences of students is *predictable chart writing*. This method, adapted from Cunningham (2001), was created by Dr. Gretchen Hanser (2006) through The Center for Literacy and Disabilities Studies at the University of Chapel Hill. Through the use of this program, experiences and thoughts are recorded on a large chart. The teacher introduces the subject and gives a title. Each student is then encouraged to give an ending to a sentence, such as "I saw _____," or "I ate _____," or "When we went to Krispy Kreme I _____."

During the following days, the sentences are reread and then cut apart into words and given to the students. These sentences, which have been cut apart into words, provide an excellent probe for assessing a child's reading level and understanding of sentence structure. To conduct this probe, just pass out the words and provide no help in the beginning. After the students are given the opportunity to reconstruct the sentence, collect data on related individualized education plan goals. Once the students are given the opportunity to reassemble the sentence, they are guided through putting the words back together to form the original sentence. Putting the words back into a sentence can be a group lesson or an individual lesson. This guidance can be further enhanced by referring to a model sentence on a large chart. It is recommended that this not be a one-time lesson. These sentences can be used over and over to teach many skills, including sight words. Once you feel you have exhausted your possibilities for using the sentences or just feel it is time to move on, the words are arranged in a sentence, and each student's sentence is glued on a large sheet of construction paper. These pages then become the pages of a book for classroom use. A picture is often included. For example, when writing about a favorite animal from the jungle, we glued pictures of the chosen animals on the page. Pictures taken with digital cameras on field trips can be printed out and glued on the pages, including pictures of students themselves involved in the activity.

These student-created books are excellent for guided reading, especially at an early reading level, due to the repetitive nature of the text.

Photo 6.8   Raising awareness of print through student-created books developed through predictable chart writing

The books are also valuable because the text is related to actual experiences, thus providing a built-in level of understanding. The books can be shared often as a group lesson. In addition, students may be given the opportunity to read a selected book aloud to the group. These books make excellent individual reading materials when placed on display in the reading corner.

WITHIN THE SCHOOL: BRINGING LITERATURE TO LIFE

When teaching a theme, our classrooms should become virtual environments of the theme. It works well to use murals and actual objects, as well as guests to bring experiences to students. Students will delight in reading in a tree house while learning about *The Swiss Family Robinson*. Reading in a boat while learning about *The Whale Rider* provides adventure. Walking into Narnia and finding Mr. Tumnus standing by a light post is sure to provide enchantment. These experiences lead to understanding, build language, and hook meaning to words.

Photo 6.9   Mr. Tumnus, a character from *The Lion, the Witch, and the Wardrobe,* helps bring literature to life in the classroom

Photo 6.10   Matthew Burrill, who portrayed Romey in *Where the Lilies Bloom*, answers questions from the students.

Photo 6.11   Staff and students hold an eighteenth-century feast after reading the many versions of *Cinderella*

Photo 6.12 A student dressed as *The Neverending Story* character Teeny Weeny

Photo 6.13 Students enjoy a belly dancer during a reading of *Aladdin*

PRESENTATIONS

Students with significant disabilities have often watched siblings, cousins, and friends work on important school projects. Family members are involved, and much attention is given to helping gather materials and pull the project together. Providing equal opportunities for individuals with special needs is rewarding not only for the student but also for the families and teachers.

Some themes lend themselves well to student presentations. Although presentations should not be assigned too frequently, it is a good idea to provide students with this experience a couple of times a year. In one of the lesson plans at the back of this book—the thematic unit "Survival" based on *Island of the Blue Dolphins*—you will find a section on presentations. This sample family letter can be used when teaching about famous women or ocean animals or as a model for other units.

Although the families of the students are asked to work with the students to prepare presentations, there is much work to be done in the classroom. In order to teach the students to give the presentations, it is best to set a due date of at least one week prior to the date they are to be given.

Once the presentations arrive at school, staff should begin to work with each individual student to prepare for the actual presentation. If a student is a reader and is verbal, then practicing the text is appropriate. If a student is verbal but reads only symbols or small bits of text, the staff must work to help structure the presentation in a way that leads to success. For these students, cue cards with picture prompts could be provided. If a student is not yet at a symbolic level, the child could present using objects attached to the screen of a communication device. For students who are nonverbal, preparation includes programming a communication device or other alternative means of presenting the information.

Students love the opportunity to have their turn in front of an audience. By looking at the individual needs of each person and structuring to assure success, this opportunity for fame will be memorable to families, students, and classroom staff.

ADVANCED ASSIGNMENTS

As has been previously stated, classrooms for students with significant disabilities are often multilevel. Some students are not able to understand sound-symbol relationships, while others read well enough to read in the content area. It is important to constantly teach skills at all levels in order to assure that students are making progress.

In the case of some literature selections, such as *The Black Stallion*, there are easy-to-read classics, written at approximately a second-grade level.

Photo 6.14   Student making a presentation about arctic animals during a theme based on *Stone Fox*

Photo 6.15   Student making a presentation on bananas during a theme based on *The Jungle Book*

These books not only provide independent reading for our more advanced students but also provide exercises in comprehension and vocabulary.

In addition to the use of the easy-to-read classics, advanced students may be given the opportunity to complete assigned research projects. While some view this as extra work, we have found this not true for our students. Most students with significant disabilities are pleased to have the chance to learn, and they find these assignments to be a fun way to learn. They actually seek the opportunity. We know that this is not the case for all students. Some students consider written assignments to be work, and they are often not welcome. It is the responsibility of each teacher to know his or her students, create fun ways for students to demonstrate knowledge, and determine the level and amount of instruction needed.

When research assignments are assigned, the students should be given a choice of several research subjects. Once a choice is made, opportunities are provided for the research on the subject. The research is done either in the library or on the Internet. After the research is completed, we provide the support needed for the student to write a report. The students work with a teacher, teaching assistant, or peer tutor to make a rough draft. After the rough draft is completed, the students are given the opportunity to type the final copy using a word processor. If communication is a challenge, alternative ways of making a presentation are employed. These alternatives usually involve technology, such as the use of computer programs that involve speech, switches, or the student's own communication device. The report is then presented to the group and becomes a learning situation not only for the student reporting but also for the entire group.

Individual, advanced assignments, such as research reports, provide the opportunity to increase both reading and writing skills. In addition, the students learn new science, social studies, and geography concepts.

Multilevel classrooms are the norm rather than the exception in special education. One answer to meeting the needs of the more advanced students is the provision of higher-level assignments to the higher-level students. By providing opportunities for creative, advanced assignments, teachers provide motivation and opportunities for success.

CONCLUDING A THEME

When the last chapter of a selection of literature has been read and all related activities are finished, it is time to bring the theme to an end. As was the case at the beginning of the unit, we conclude with an air of celebration. This celebration is usually simple and may be nothing more than the singing of favorite songs, the reading of poetry, or a party with a specially decorated cake.

A last viewing of the related movie is always a part of the final celebration. Students enjoy the opportunity to once again view the movie. As the viewing takes place, it is done through the eyes of individuals who are now much more likely to understand the plot, be able to name the characters, or discuss the setting. The literature selection has become a part of the students, just as good literature becomes a part of each of us in special ways.

Photo 6.16   End of theme celebration: a cookie made by Lewis

INSTRUCTIONAL DELIVERY: A CHECKLIST

❏ Set up classroom, theme, and individual schedules
❏ Make lesson plans for an exciting introduction to the theme
❏ Introduce the book and show the entire video or DVD
❏ Introduce vocabulary
❏ Begin reading the book and showing the video or DVD chapter by chapter
❏ Follow the reading of each chapter with a group retelling lesson
❏ Provide opportunities for presentations of advanced assignments
❏ Celebration

7 Home Involvement

Teacher Objectives

- Emphasize parent-school communication to help parents understand the importance of reviewing work from school
- Emphasize the importance of a review of the retelling and vocabulary at home to help with retention and comprehension
- Share how the student presentations give students a chance to work with families and share their information with other classmates

In Chapter 1, "Research and Program Overview," it was noted that one of the key characteristics of theme teaching is to find ways to involve students' families. In the "Building a Theme" section, it was noted that parent-school communication is very important. As in general education, parental involvement varies from student to student. Many students in special education have never been taught using themes. It is so different from worksheets and work jobs that parents need as much information as possible to understand what is going on in the classroom. Many students have also never had homework, so parents may need information regarding the importance of reviewing work from school.

It is important for teachers to keep in mind that homework is designed for students to practice material that was already taught in the classroom. Teachers need to be aware and understand that families are also living with the complex demands of parenting a child with a disability. There may be times when families cannot offer the support needed for the student to practice content. Keeping a balance between a reasonable amount of material to practice and quality family time is crucial for maintaining a productive relationship with the family.

SHARING THE RETELLING

As discussed in Chapter 6, "Instructional Delivery," the retelling of a story is a very important way for students to learn about the story and the beginning reading process. Each day during a theme, after the story has been retold, it is typed in a large and readable font. Comic Sans (Microsoft Word) with a size 20 font is used because the font is close to actual print. The entry is then added to a folder (with three-hole clasps) with the theme title on the front. A color copy of the front of the book or the video can also be used as a front cover and adds a nice touch to the theme book. This booklet is sent home every day to be reviewed. Parents are invited to read the new chapter with their child and review the previous entries. Parents are also encouraged to let their child read as much of the entry as possible and point out different letters. When a letter sound is emphasized during theme time by highlighting it, parents are asked to review that particular letter at home. This immersion into the theme and retelling of the story at school and at home accelerates learning and the reading process. Practice at home also facilitates generalization of the skills beyond the classroom. At the end of a theme, the book is taken out of the folder and is bound so the students can take the retelling home. If there are six themes during the year, the students have added six adapted books to their library at home.

For students whose families are not able to participate, staff members read to them during self-selected reading or leisure time, or peer tutors volunteer to reread the story to the students. The retelling is also put on an IntelliTools Classroom Suite Activity Page or PowerPoint (see the PowerTalk link in the "Web Resources," in the Resources) program so students can listen to it and read along at independent reading time or at leisure.

SHARING THE VOCABULARY

The vocabulary words for the unit are also copied in alphabetical order and sent home in the book with the student. This is another area where review helps cement the idea that letters together make words. Parents are encouraged to review the words in flashcard style and also work on definitions. Simple directions to the parents to begin reviewing the vocabulary are to match the word with the symbol. The parents say, "Here is the word *creek*. Show me the picture of the creek." As the child progresses, the process can be reversed, such as, "Here is a picture of a creek. Can you show me the word *creek*?" Suggestions are also provided, including when referring to a word such as *island*, to ask, "What is a word that means land surrounded by water?" Another suggestion is to review the words by using a time-delay method. The parents place the cards on a table or the floor and ask,

"Show me the word _____." Give ample amounts of time to begin with (especially for students with autism), and decrease the time as the student becomes more familiar with the words. If the child gets the answer wrong, instruct the parents to say, "That is the word _____. Can you show me the word _____?" instead of saying the previous answer was wrong. That way, words can be reviewed, it is a continuous learning process, and the child can feel successful. If the child gets the answer right, instruct the parent to praise the child and say, "You're right! This word is _____."

As we first started sending home homework and doing the time delay method, we were so excited when many of our students who are nonverbal began giving us the definitions by using communication systems. We found they knew the information; they just were not able to tell us the answers because they did not have the means.

PRESENTATIONS

When parents are asked to help with presentations, there will also be differ ent levels of participation. Overall, we found that most parents help with the research and making of the posters or booklets. Many of our students have Medicaid funding and have a Community Alternatives Placement worker that works on goals at home or in the community. This person can help with homework and also do activities such as going to the library and working on a presentation. This coordinates well with a student's community goals. Presentations are also a great way staff can work with students.

As in general-education classes, there may be families who want to do all of the work for their child. We have found that when the emphasis is placed on allowing students the opportunity to show what they can do and stating the presentations are for that purpose and not a grade, the participation of the student increases.

In the Sample Lesson Plans and Related Resources section, in the theme materials for *Island of the Blue Dolphins*, there is a parent letter about presentations. This gives some detailed information about what is expected. Be sure to let parents know that help with communication devices will be provided if needed.

Parents are invited to come to school on the day of presentations. There were not many dry eyes in our classroom the first time the students made presentations. Parents, staff, and administration were thrilled the students were having the chance to share with others what they had learned. They were making presentations just like their peers in general-education classes. The more presentations that were done, the more comfortable the students became, leading to even more meaningful and informational presentations.

HOME INVOLVEMENT: A CHECKLIST

❏ Create folder for retelling entries
❏ Type entries and send home in folders on a daily basis
❏ Copy the vocabulary words, and place in folder to send home
❏ Suggest theme-related activities parents or caregivers can do with the students
❏ If presentations are being done during the theme, send home information on how parents or caregivers can assist the students

8 Assessment

- Utilize individual journaling to assess comprehension
- Develop individualized education plan (IEP) goals based on the standard course of study (SCS) related to theme-based activities
- Apply graphing methods to lessons and instruct students in analyzing data
- Incorporate games into activities assessing learning

As with any course of study or teaching method, assessment is a mandatory part of the process in special education. It has been noted that students who have teachers who monitor progress and revise their instructional plans according to student needs progress at a faster rate than those whose teachers do not (Stecker & Fuchs, 2000). It is very important to continually monitor student progress so you can find out what is and what is not working with your students. We have found that teaching through themes gives us many different ways to assess the progress of our students.

INDIVIDUAL JOURNALING

After reading a chapter and completing group retelling, students are given their own journal and asked to describe what they just heard or learned. A spiral-bound book with blank, sturdy paper (similar to card stock) is used. Questions such as, "What was the most important thing that happened in the chapter?" or "What was your favorite thing that happened in the book?" are asked. The journal is then given to the student, along with pencils, markers, crayons, and so on, and he or she is asked to write or draw in the book. Much further information is not given because the students should come up with their own ideas. If the student has a physical disability that makes it difficult to write or draw, staff can do hand-over-hand assistance, or the students can tell (through words or communication devices or communication notebooks) what they want to write or draw. The students should be allowed to use their own alternative pencil (see Chapter 5).

When the theme "Courage" using *The Wizard of Oz* was done, there were wonderful drawings of Dorothy, the yellow brick road, and the other characters in the story. One student put the letter "M" all over the page. When asked to describe his drawing, he said, "Flying monkeys." After working on the *Heidi* theme one day, a drawing by one of the students was found on her desk. During leisure time, she had copied some of a story one of the teachers had created. It had a house with stones around it and an animal with a smiley face. It also had the letters, "Heidi went to Grandfatetr's [Grandfather's] House" on it. The amount of comprehension that comes through with this type of activity is amazing.

Photo 8.1 A student's demonstration of emergent literacy skills shown by writing M's for flying monkeys from *The Wizard of Oz*

Photo 8.2 A student's demonstration of the awareness of print following the reading of a chapter from *Heidi*

Photo 8.3 Journaling demonstrating more advanced written expression and comprehension

ADDRESSING THE STANDARD COURSE OF STUDY

In North Carolina, as in the rest of the nation, IEPs are written for each student. We have found that many of the goals in the IEPs relate to theme and can easily be embedded in instruction. (See chart below for IEP goal ideas). Using goals in this way helps cut down on paperwork time. Staff members bring data sheets to theme time to collect data as needed, and this helps bring more IEP goals into the theme process.

For the past few years, North Carolina has placed a strong emphasis on aligning IEP goals with the SCS. Since our students are significantly below grade level, extensions of the SCS are used as the foundation for instruction. Extensions of the SCS in North Carolina are found at http://www.ncpublicschools.org/curriculum/ncecs. Thematic instruction is an excellent way to connect goals to the SCS.

Examples of IEP Goals Aligned With the Extension of the Standard Course of Study

1. English/language arts, 6th grade, competency Goal 1: The learner will use language to express individual perspectives drawn from personal or related experience.

   IEP Goal: Using a communication device, sign language, or words, Gordon will indicate how a passage from a book makes him feel (happy, sad, scared, etc.).

2. English/language arts, 8th grade, competency Goal 6: The learner will extend vocabulary knowledge by learning and using new words.

   IEP Goal: Given 10 vocabulary words, Eric will correctly match each word to a corresponding symbol.

3. Math, 8th grade, competency Goal 1: The learner will develop number sense for real numbers.

   IEP Goal: Given a journal entry, Nick will count the number of highlighted letters, up to 10 letters.

4. English/language arts, 7th grade, competency Goal 2: The learner will explore, interact with, and demonstrate comprehension of information materials that are read, heard, or viewed.

   IEP Goal: Given 10 vocabulary words, Casey will answer comprehension questions about a story or event.

DATA COLLECTION

Because the task of data collection can be time consuming, it is important to find ways during the regular course of the day in which to collect data necessary to measure students' progress toward their goals. During theme time, there are a number of ways to collect data. Each students' theme-related data sheet can be put on a clipboard or in the back of the communication book for easy access. If the goal is about vocabulary, the student or staff can mark a correctly answered word (with an erasable marker) directly on the laminated theme pages in the communication book, and the data can be transferred to the data sheet. Following are examples of real goals and data sheets used with our students for identifying letters (Table 8.1) and vocabulary words (Table 8.2) and answering comprehension questions (Table 8.3). These graphs can simply be used to track students' progress by entering dates and checkmarks in the squares. However, we wanted to record more specific information about the extent and circumstances of students' learning, and developed a code to do so. Our data codes are in the shaded box below and may be useful to you as you develop your own system for keeping track of IEP goals.

Student Response Codes	"Where" Codes		"With Whom" Codes	
+ correct	BR bathroom	MC media center	A Administrator	PT physical therapist
- incorrect	CA cafeteria		GET gen. ed. teacher	SLP speech pathologist
X did not attempt	CL classroom	R restaurant	I student intern	
I independent	FT field trip	S store	N nurse	OT occupational therapist
G gestural	G gym	TR therapy room	P peer	
NV nonspecific verbal	GEC general ed. class	O other	T teacher	TA (1-4) teacher assistant
V verbal	H home	AC (1-4) alternate classroom	PA parent	
M model			S substitute	O other
P partial physical		SO school office		V volunteer
F full physical				ST spec. teacher (music, art, p.e.)

Attendance Codes				
AB absent	NS no school	H hospital	O other	W weather

Table 8.1 IEP Goals Data Sheet for Letters. During retelling, Anni is asked, "What letter makes the _____ sound?" If Anni points to the correct letter, a check is made on the data sheet.

IEP Goals Data Sheet for Letters

Student: Anni **Standard Course of Study** **Goal for Reading:** English/Language Arts, Competency #6		**Goal:** Anni will identify the correct letter for 15 consonant sounds.					
Schedule or → **Dates** **Activity ↓**							
	B						
	C						
	D						
	F						
	H						
	J						
	L						
	M						
	N						
	P						
	R						
	S						
	T						
	V						
	W						
Number Correct							
Where							
With Whom							
Material Used							

Table 8.2 IEP Goals Data Sheet for Vocabulary for Angelica

IEP Goals Data Sheet for Vocabulary

Student: Angelica **Standard Course of Study Goal for Reading:** English/Language Arts, Competency #6		**Goal:** Given 20 vocabulary words, Angelica will learn/identify the definitions of 20 out of 20 of the words.					
Vocabulary Activity	**Dates**						
1. stallion							
2. rescue							
3. determination							
4. stable							
5. shipwreck							
6. race							
7. stormy							
8. beach							
9. saddle							
10. mane							
11. worried							
12. potato							
13. taxes							
14. race							
15. winter							
16. sled							
17. sadness							
18. died							
19. cold							
20. win							
Number Correct							
Where							
With Whom							
Material Used							

Table 8.3 IEP Goals Data Sheet for Comprehension Questions for Kendall

IEP Goals Data Sheet for Comprehension Questions

Student: Kendall
Standard Course of Study Goal for Math:
Reading Competency Goal #4

Goal: Given a selection of text, Kendall will answer "What happened?" What happened next?" and "What do you think will happen next?" comprehension questions.

Date												
What Happened?												
What Happened Next?												
What Do You Think Will Happen Next?												
Number Correct												
Where												
With Whom												
Date												
What Happened?												
What Happened Next?												
What Do You Think Will Happen Next?												
Number Correct												
Where												
With Whom												

GRAPHING

Graphing exercises have increased our students' math skills as well as helped in assessing comprehension. There are many opportunities for graphing! Initially, it was used it as a way to find out what the favorite themes were during the year. The books were placed in a line, and, using the name boxes to call out names, each student was given the opportunity to place his or her name above a favorite book. The students were able to visually assess which book was the classroom favorite, and we used it as a math exercise, asking, "Which book has more names above it? Which has the least?"

Graphing is now incorporated into every theme and into many activities. When teaching the theme, "Courage," using *The Wizard of Oz*, the number of Skittles (the candy advertised as having the colors of the rainbow) found in a bag were graphed (see *The Wizard of Oz* Lesson Plan, "Graphing Skittles"). In that theme, each student's birthstone was graphed, and the students found that the majority of them were born in September (see Photo 4.5). In the theme using *Island of the Blue Dolphins*, the students sorted shells and graphed the results. In the theme using *These Happy, Golden Years*, the students gathered items from the woods and graphed items they had found, such as pine needles, stones, moss, leaves, and acorns. In the theme using *Stone Fox*, the amount of miles a musher and his dog team went in the Iditarod was graphed. Graphing exercises can be added to almost any lesson, and the students soon learn and understand the graphing process. An IEP goal for this could be "Using bar graphs or pictographs, Eli will collect, organize, and display data. SCS Extensions: 8th grade math Goal 4: The student will collect, organize, and display data to solve problems" (see Table 8.4).

Table 8.4 IEP Goals Data Sheet for Math

IEP Goals Data Sheet for Math

Student: Eli **Standard Course of Study Goal for Math:** Math Competency Goal #4										**Goal:** Using bar graphs or pictographs, Eli will collect, organize, and display data.	
Date											
Collect Data											
Organize Data											
Display on Graphs											
Number Correct											
Where											
With Whom											
Date											
Collect Data											
Organize Data											
Display on Graphs											
Number Correct											
Where											
With Whom											

RETELLING AS ASSESSMENT

In Chapter 6, much emphasis is given to retelling and to the ways it can be used to judge student understanding and comprehension. Because the value of retelling cannot be overemphasized, it is suggested that teachers reread the retelling information when planning for assessment.

ADAPTIVE PROGRAMS

Adaptive programs such as Classroom Suite from IntelliTools can be excellent tools for assessing students who have difficulty with verbal and written expression. This is a great way to see whether your students understand the book. It is also a good way to get baseline information and do pre- or posttests to assess learning. As you will note, the questions are written in fill-in-the-blank form with the vocabulary words with pictures on the side or top for the students to complete. For higher-level readers, you can also use words without the pictures. Our students often choose this program for a leisure activity, and it can be used for independent reading time. This program is very beneficial for assessing learning (see IntelliTools Classroom Suite questions included in the Sample Lesson Plans and Related Resources section).

GAMES

Anytime a teacher can incorporate a game into a lesson makes the lesson more fun for the students and easier for the teacher. One of the first games we used was provided by our speech pathologist. She called it the "I have— Who has" game, and it is used in every unit with the vocabulary words. Two vocabulary words with the symbols are put on a 2" × 3" card with the words and symbols "I have" and "Who has" printed on them.

Each child is given a card until all the cards are given out, so some students may get more than one according to how many students are in the class. There is a sticker on the back of one of the cards indicating who goes first. For instance, the first student reads his card, and the other students have to listen to see if he calls out a word on their card. "I have *promise*. Who has *herb*?" Then the student who had *herb* would say, "I have *herb*. Who has *quilt*?" and each card would be read until all words are covered. This game is especially fun after the students have done it for a while and it is done with more rhythm. This helps in assessing the identification of words. Communication devices are used for nonverbal students.

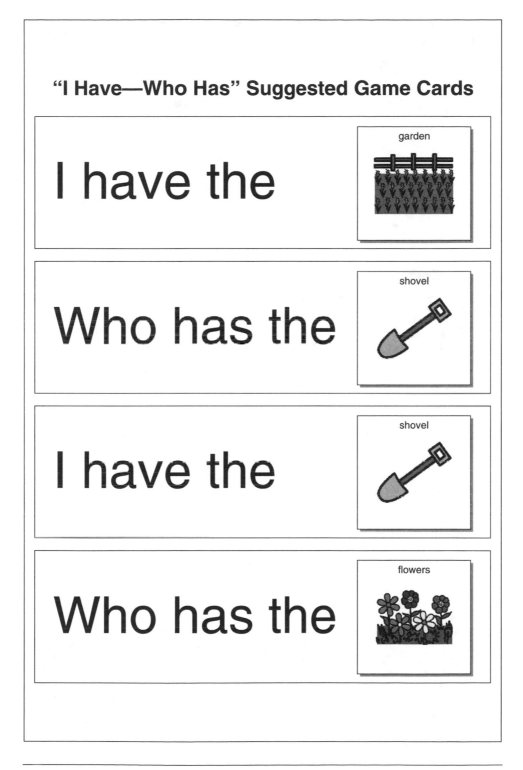

"I Have—Who Has" Suggested Game Cards

I have the · garden

Who has the · shovel

I have the · shovel

Who has the · flowers

Photo 8.4

Photo 8.5   Matching vocabulary to books in a group comprehension lesson. This activity demonstrated retention of vocabulary and the connection to certain literature selections covered over the course of one school year.

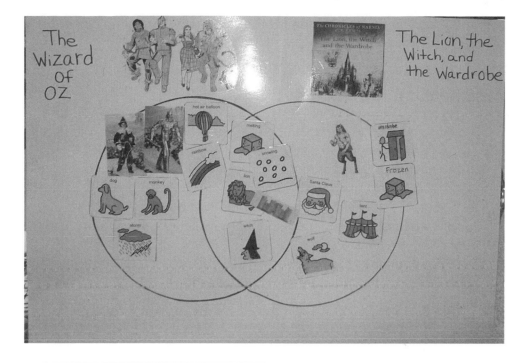

Photo 8.6   Students show comprehension through a Venn diagram comparing *The Wizard of Oz* and *The Lion, the Witch, and the Wardrobe.*

Another game we play with vocabulary words helps assess comprehension. It is the simple, "I'm thinking of a word..." and is used with each of the vocabulary words. For example, we would say, "I'm thinking of a word that is the color of the city Dorothy, Scarecrow, the Lion, and the Tin Man went to." The students then use their communication devices or voices to call out the answer.

Bingo with vocabulary words is also an easy way to assess the identification of the words. Boardmaker has a program that helps make bingo games from symbols (see sample bingo card in the Sample Lesson Plans and Related Resources section).

At the beginning of theme time, we choose a vocabulary word and play a game similar to "Wheel of Fortune." A board is used with card pockets (such as the cards that go in library books) taped to it. Letters of the alphabet are laminated on index cards, which can be inserted into the card pockets. Names are drawn from the name box, and students then guess the letters. After two letters are guessed, the students are allowed to try to guess the word. A bell is used for correct answers and a communication device with a student saying "annnhhhh!" for incorrect answers. This game helps assess phonemic awareness and understanding as well as letter and vocabulary identification. We also use "Wheel of

Fortune" to enhance anticipation for the next theme by giving clues about the title or characters' names.

ASSESSMENT: A CHECKLIST

☐ Offer journaling opportunities to assess comprehension and feelings about a chapter or book

☐ Based on individual student needs, create IEP goals related to theme activities and linked to the SCS

☐ Use graphing exercises to expand math and literacy lessons

☐ Use retelling to assess understanding of letters, vocabulary words, and comprehension

☐ Use computer programs such as IntelliTools Classroom Suite for students to answer comprehension questions

☐ Develop games to assess understanding of vocabulary words

Inclusion and Collaboration With General Education Teachers

Teacher Objective

♦ Create ways to work with special education, inclusion, and general education teachers.

*G*eneral education refers to the classes in school other than special education. *Inclusion* refers to the collaboration between general education and special education teachers. As previously stated, thematic teaching has been used in general education classes for years. It has been a process to learn how the thematic units can be incorporated into the general education and inclusion classes, and it has been well worth the effort.

There is a push in the United States for more students to be incorporated into the general education classroom. As a result, students with more severe disabilities are in the general education classrooms. This book is a planning book for teachers who are working with students in self-contained classes or included in general education classrooms. As students with disabilities become more integrated, the information in this book will become more of a priority to special education teachers.

SPECIAL EDUCATION TEACHERS WORKING WITH GENERAL EDUCATION TEACHERS

When we first started our theme-based instruction, we realized we were going to need assistance from the general education teachers in our school. In Chapter 3, "Building a Theme," we discussed how we worked with the media specialist in our schools to find age-appropriate material for our students. After talking with her, we asked our school principal if we could meet with the teachers from each grade. He was very receptive and helped set up meetings with the teachers. We sent out invitations with e-mail reminders and asked the teachers to come to one of our rooms to discuss how we used technology within our theme-based instruction. Since we were reading *Stone Fox* at the time, we provided potato chip cookies, which we made with our students because potatoes were grown on the farm in the story. We spent about 30 minutes discussing how we were teaching. The teachers were very supportive and gave us some good suggestions.

Because of those initial meetings, teachers asked to work with us and our students. We partnered with a seventh-grade classroom. Before the partnership, we went to the general education classroom to discuss different types of disabilities and answer questions the students had. Our students gave presentations to the classroom, and students from that classroom read stories they developed to our students.

Cinderella was actually chosen because the general education class was reading many different versions of the story and developing stories of their own. They shared the books and stories, and we ended up with about 25 different versions of the story! There was an Appalachian version, one from Texas, and a Native American version. Even though we initially thought *Cinderella* would be too juvenile, it turned out to be a very enriching unit. The seventh-grade classroom was invited to our Royal Ball at the end of the theme.

During the unit based on *My Side of the Mountain*, we played a game where students from both classrooms answered different questions from the book. It was very exciting when one of our students helped a general education student answer a question correctly! This partnership added a great deal to our themes, and we would strongly encourage working with a general education classroom. The students from the general education classroom learned from our students and became more comfortable with and accepting of our students with disabilities.

Thematic teaching lends itself to teaching students with different ability levels. One of the teachers we talked to about our program felt that it was a matter of confidence and flexibility on the teachers' (both general education and special education) part to make the integration and inclusion of students possible.

Here are some examples of ways to work with general education classroom teachers in your school:

1. If a teacher is reading a particular book in class, ask if it is possible to join in for some related activities. If a relationship has already been established with a teacher, suggest a book to read together. Classes can also watch the initial showing of the video together.

2. At the end of a chapter, structure a game similar to "Quiz Bowl." Create questions from the chapter geared toward each ability level. Students can have communication devices to answer questions or can work with a buddy on the questions. Students can ring a bell when they have the answer or use their devices.

3. Integrate other subjects into the theme. Just as our students have to follow extensions of the standard course of study (SCS), general education students and teachers are also under a great deal of pressure to follow it. All students can be a part of the process. One way to do this is to use a science lesson dealing with the five senses (in the seventh-grade SCS) and combine it with a literacy lesson. During *Stone Fox* and the theme of "Winter," students went outside and noticed things with their senses (hearing the howling wind, the smell of smoke, seeing snow blowing, touching the ice, tasting snow cream, etc.). When they came in, they wrote haiku from what they had noticed. This would be a great way to combine classes and create poems or other literary pieces.

4. While working with bubble maps or graphic organizers (seventh-grade SCS), general education students, alongside students from special education or inclusion classes, would create the actual map or organizer about a particular theme. They would work with the special education students by being the "leader" of the discussion and brainstorm ideas about the topic. Teachers from both classes would facilitate the groups and assist as needed.

5. Create artwork together. When our classes were reading *My Side of the Mountain*, the general education class made quilt squares by drawing a scene from the story and writing a paragraph about it. Our students used images from the Internet they chose or colored in pages of animals they liked from the story. What they wanted to tell about the picture was transcribed and written on the squares. Students with disabilities could be paired with nondisabled peers during this process.

As a special education teacher facilitating inclusion, you can work with your general education education teacher who is doing a theme. Here are some suggestions:

- Program communication devices so that students will be ready to communicate on the first day of the theme
- Pair symbols with vocabulary words for students who do not read at grade level
- Break up reading passages into smaller units if your students are feeling overwhelmed by the materials
- Use assistive technology devices to help with accommodations such as testing outside of the room or read-aloud situations

If you are a general education teacher, you are already adapting materials in your classroom to meet the needs of your diverse students. Use this book as a guide for making adaptations to your thematic units.

PEER TUTORS

Our program has worked with peer tutors for many years. Peer tutors are students from general education who take a class and get credit for working with our students. Because of the different levels of our classrooms, the peer tutors have different types of assignments. Some peer tutors support students during lunch, and others read with and to our students. The peer tutors in our classes have assignments that are usually based on themes. These assignments enriched our themes. Our peer tutors have made ruby red slippers for *The Wizard of Oz* theme and posters of *The Black Stallion*. They made illustrated condensed books based on the current theme and have worked with students learning vocabulary words. Peer tutors give students a chance to interact with general education students. It is a two-way learning experience because most of the general education students say they benefit from the class. Some of our peer tutors go on to college to become special education teachers. It is a program that benefits all the students involved.

Photo 9.1   A peer tutor and a student practice reading a predictable chart page

GENERAL EDUCATION: A CHECKLIST

☐ Meet with the principal and discuss using a thematic approach with students

☐ Meet with the media specialist and grade-level teachers and discuss the thematic approach

☐ Ask for suggestions from general education teachers for age-appropriate books they have used and enjoyed; think of specific areas in which students could be involved in the general education classroom

☐ Discuss the possibility of a peer-tutoring program with the principal and other teachers who are interested

10 Functional Skills

♦ Incorporate functional skills throughout the school day

Functional skills usually relate to basic skills, employment, and independent living. For many years in special education, functional skills were the focus of individual education plan (IEP) goals and instruction. As previously stated, government mandates, parents, and our own interest in increasing literacy skills led us to focus more on academics while still incorporating functional goals for our students.

TEACHING SKILLS THROUGHOUT THE DAY

Many functional skills incorporate academic skills such as reading and math skills. Examples of functional skills taught throughout the day and connected to theme follow.

Cooking	In every theme, there is a cooking activity included in the lesson plans. Incorporated into the activity are reading and math. All of the recipes are written on a flip chart. Symbols and words are used for the directions, such as *stir, pour, measure,* and *bake.* Cooking activities also incorporate following directions and sequencing events. Every student participates in the activity, whether it is to set the oven, stir, or measure.

Cleaning	Cleaning is done as needed as it naturally occurs during the day. If someone spills something, he or she is taught how to clean it up. There is usually cleaning time on most Fridays, and every student is assigned an area to straighten. Different students clean the lunch table. When we do cooking activities, students often help clean up the kitchen. Doing these things as they come up naturally makes it more meaningful for the students.
Personal Hygiene	Again, this is something that is done throughout the day. There is a schedule for bathroom time, but students who have accidents receive assistance with cleanup. A student who needs a shower is given as much assistance as needed to access the facilities. A student whose clothes get messy is taught to use the washing machine and dryer (this also occurs after swimming). During these times, ways to keep clean are discussed, and a checklist with symbols is made if needed. Teaching this way allows for more individual instruction in a meaningful setting.
Time/Time Clock/Calendar	Schedules are reviewed every morning with the students. Boardmaker symbols are paired with words and times for each activity. For students who read well, a schedule with words only is made. Again, telling time becomes a natural part of the day. We make statements such as, "It's 9:00, time for group" and "It's 11:30, time for lunch." For students who are working on time specifically, they are asked what time it is and what activity we should be doing. Personal calendars are used to let students know what activities are occurring in the theme. Students write down activities on the calendar. They also put events and activities in their own lives that are interesting to them.
Write Name	Students are asked to sign in during group time and other times during the day. For those who do not write, stamps are used. This helps the students practice writing their name and also gives the other students in the class familiarity with their classmate's written name. In the community, it is very natural to be asked for a signature for something, so the students can feel they are more a part of the world around them.
Money	Field trips are an excellent time to teach money skills in the real world, as the students pay for food at restaurants, buy tickets to events, or purchase such items as vegetables at a farmers' market.

When we first began theme-based instruction, other teachers in our program asked, "When do you teach functional skills?" Our program has been functionally based for years. Our response to these teachers was that we believe teaching functional skills throughout the day is more meaningful than doing it in isolation. It makes more sense to teachers and students to teach skills as the opportunity arises rather than to practice tying shoes or washing hands at a scheduled time of the day.

Sample Lesson Plans and Related Resources

T hese resources are intended to assist you in your instruction and assessment. Please feel free to use or adapt the lesson plans to suit your students' needs, and to copy the reproducible forms if they will be helpful in your teaching.

Weekly Thematic Lesson Plan   **108**

To be used as a model for the integration of a thematic unit into instruction over the course of a week.

Thematic Unit Planning Sheet   **119**

A bubble map used for planning. See Chapter 3, under "Planning," for more information about the graphic organizer.

Standard Course of Study Planning Sheet   **120**

To help with making connections to the standard course of study, the importance of which is also discussed in Chapter 3.

Lesson Plans   **121**

These sample lesson plans were designed to provide a guide and materials for thematic instruction. Each set of lesson plans includes a Thematic Unit Planning Sheet, a summary of the story, lesson plans, vocabulary, and a communication board. The vocabulary and communication board are designed to be easily reproduced and laminated for student use. In addition, for The Black Stallion *lesson plan, we've included sample bingo game cards and a set of comprehension questions designed with Classroom Suite, an IntelliTools program: see Chapter 8.*

> *The Black Stallion* Lesson Plan
> *Island of the Blue Dolphins* Lesson Plan
> *Where the Lillies Bloom* Lesson Plan
> *Stone Fox* Lesson Plan
> *The Wizard of Oz* Lesson Plan

Assistive Technology Planning Sheet   **185**

To help plan and prepare the technology needed for individual students (see Chapter 4).

Activites: Comprehension and Vocabulary   **186**

Instructions for creating these learning activities using IntelliTools

Weekly Thematic Lesson Plan

This plan may be used as a model for the integration of a thematic unit into instruction over the course of a week. It shows how a theme can be used as conceptual glue to strengthen bonds to knowledge and interrelate subjects such as math, art, writing, functional skills, social studies, and science throughout the day.

This set of plans relates to the theme "Winter," using *Stone Fox*. If you look at the letter to the parents in Chapter 3, you will see that many of the activities in these plans relate to the activities listed for the week of March 10–14. If you look at March 12 in the family letter, you will see that the parent letter stated that we would do an art lesson using potatoes. If you look at Monday in this set of plans, the first lesson is self-selected reading. If you refer back to Table 4.1, you will see that self-selected reading occurs at 9:15 on Mondays.

WINTER

Monday

Self-Selected Reading

Self-selected reading is a time when students choose and enjoy the books that they would like to read. These books may be either theme-related books or other books in the classroom library.

After the reading of *Owl Moon* (Yolen, 1987) the book should be available for self-selected reading. In addition, other theme-related books, both fiction and nonfiction, should be present in the classroom for the enjoyment of individuals. Students may also select from classroom-made books such as copies of previous literature retellings or books made from predictable chart writing.

Writing Mini Lesson: Model Journaling

Last week the class enjoyed a trip to Krispy Kreme Doughnuts and the potato bar at Ryan's Steak House. Pictures were taken using digital cameras. In addition, students were able to collect items for their writing boxes. The following lesson demonstrates how to use the community experience for teaching language arts skills. (See Planning for Community Experiences in Chapter 3.)

Materials

- Chart paper
- Souvenir or picture from the field trip to Krispy Kreme and Ryan's Steak House
- Marker

Instructions

1. Connect to prior learning by talking about the trip and the many things they did and saw.
2. Model a journal entry using a photo or souvenir from the trip.
3. Use a large piece of chart paper and record your thoughts as you think out loud. You could even draw a picture to model journaling for students who are at an emergent level.
4. Read the journal entry to the students and then introduce the students to the following lesson.

Students Write: Student Journaling

In this lesson, students are given the opportunity to record a journal entry of their own. Accept the personal spelling of the students. Remember, we want them to be able and willing to write for functional purposes and do not want them to be bogged down in worrying about spelling. This concern could limit their willingness to write. If at a later date you want to work on correct spelling, punctuation, and capitalization, editing skills may be taught.

Some students will be able to use paper and pencil, some may need to use a conventional or adapted keyboard, and others may need to work through a scribe. For more information on how to use alternative pencils, refer to Chapter 5 of this book, "Providing Access Through Assistive Technology."

Materials

- Communication books
- Individual word wall folders
- Adapted equipment as needed, including alternative ways of writing

Instructions

1. Students should be instructed to write about the trip.
2. If students are having a difficult time coming up with a topic, encourage them to look in their writing boxes for items or photos from the previous week's field trip.

3. If assessing, do not lend assistance other than serving as a scribe or facilitating the use of alternative pencils.

4. Give the students the opportunity to share their journal entries with their classmates.

Theme Time

Theme time is time set aside at least three days of the week for large-group theme instruction. It is during this time that the literature selection and vocabulary are taught, as well as other theme-related lessons.

Word Game

1. Begin theme time with a word game using the word *winter*.

2. The lesson for theme time today is the reading of Chapter 5 of *Stone Fox* (Gardiner, 2003) and a vocabulary lesson. All students will have their own communication systems available as well as the communication notebooks.

Note: Instructions for the word game that is similar to Wheel of Fortune are in Chapter 8, "Assessment," of this book.

Chapter Read-Aloud

1. Connect to prior learning and assess comprehension of the previous chapter by questioning.

2. Read aloud the retelling of the previous chapter.

3. Ask students for predictions about the next chapter.

4. Read the new chapter aloud.

5. Show the corresponding chapter of the movie. Remember to stop the movie as needed to explain information and help students make connections.

6. Lead the students in the retelling of the chapter as the teacher records the journal entry.

Sample Retelling

See Chapter 6, "Instructional Delivery," for sample retelling.

Vocabulary Lesson

Materials

Three sets of vocabulary will be used for this lesson. One is displayed on a bulletin board in the theme area, one is whole and ready for teacher use, and the last has been cut to separate the symbol from the word and is for student use. Because the vocabulary is relatively new to the students, the goal is word and symbol recognition.

Instructions

1. Pass out the vocabulary cards using the set that is for student use. Some students will receive only words; some will receive words and pictures. As the words and symbols are being distributed, it is important to think about the reading level and goals of each individual student.

2. Choose a word from the stack of cards that is for teacher use. Do not let the students see the chosen word.

3. Ask, "Who has the picture of _____?" Once the student holding the picture has answered, prompt the student to say, "I have _____." Walk to the student to get the picture, or have the student bring the picture to you.

4. Ask, "Who has the word _____?" Once the student holding the picture has answered, prompt the student to say, "I have _____." Walk to the student to get the word, or have the student bring the word to you.

5. Once you have both the word and the symbol, match them together in front of the group so that students have an opportunity to see the connection of the word to the symbol and meaning to the word.

6. Continue until all words have been matched to the appropriate symbol.

Math Graphing

This is week two of following the Iditarod. Last week each class chose a musher to track. The results are being graphed on a bar graph. Today, Jeff and Eli will be the ones to go to the Internet and find information on how far the mushers have traveled.

Materials

- Computer with Internet access
- Ongoing graph tracking the Iditarod mushers
- Markers
- Prior to the lesson, Anissa and Luke will access the Internet and find recent news on the Iditarod. Assistance will be given when needed.

Instructions

1. Connect to prior learning by reviewing the graph and pointing out information about which musher is winning.

2. Ask if anyone has been following the race in the news and provide an opportunity for sharing.

3. Ask Jeff and Eli to come forward to the area where the graph is displayed.

4. Ask Jeff to tell the distance traveled by the musher selected by his class.

5. Assist Jeff with recording the mileage on graph.

6. Ask Eli to tell the distance traveled by the musher selected by his class.

7. Assist Eli with recording the mileage on graph.

8. After the information is recorded, lead the group in a discussion about which musher is winning and a discussion of the number of miles traveled.

Tuesday

Self-Selected Reading

See the self-selected reading plans for Monday.

Calendar and Writing Skills

This lesson is used to teach both functional time skills and the language arts skill of list making. In part one, the students will use individual planners or calendars to find dates and record future events. In part two, the students will learn to make a list.

Calendar Skills

Materials

- Individual calendars
- Pencils
- Model calendar

Instructions

1. Instruct students to take out their individual calendars.

2. Connect to prior learning by having students find the month of March and by talking about the fact that presentations will be given, for example, on March 19 and 20.

3. Through questioning, lead the students into locating the dates on which presentations are to be given.

4. Talk about the fact that we are inviting families to come see the presentations so we need to make a list of who will give presentations on March 19 and who will give presentations on March 20.

5. Teach calendar skills by asking on what days of the week the 19th and 20th fall.

Writing Mini Lesson: List Making

Materials

- Chart paper
- Markers
- Pre-prepared sticky notes with names for students who may be unable to write

Instructions

1. Connect to prior knowledge by talking about the presentations, the dates on which they occur, and the need to decide who will present on what day.

2. On a large chart paper record, make two columns, one labeled Wednesday, March 19, and one labeled Thursday, March 20.

3. Invite students to come forward and write their names under the date they choose to present. For students who are unable to write, have their names already written on a sticky note that can be attached to the chart or provide the chance to spell for a scribe either by using a communication device, speaking the letters, or by pointing out the letters.

4. Tell the students that we will now be able to write an invitation to their friends and families, inviting them to come to the presentations. This will be done on Thursday during writing time.

One-on-One Instruction or Center Time

Practicing Presentations/Center Time

1. Instruct students to either work on independent work or go to an assigned center.

2. Give teaching assistants a list of the students with whom to practice presentations.

3. Each staff person will work with one student at a time preparing the voice output devices, cue cards, and other materials needed for the presentations.

Language Arts Activity

Last week the students were led in a predictable chart-writing activity about winter. The beginning of the sentence was, "In the winter, I _____." The sentences have been cut apart into words. Today, we will practice putting the sentences back together. Among skills taught in this lesson are word recognition, punctuation, and sentence structure.

Predictable Chart Writing—Making Sentences

1. Give students their cut-up sentences and a large piece of construction paper.

2. Connect to prior learning by reminding the students of the chart writing that they had done previously and sharing a model sentence that says, "In the winter, I like to _____."

3. Instruct the students to practice putting the words back together into a sentence. Give students the opportunity to independently complete the task. Take a probe to assess skills.

4. Once the probe is completed, work with individual students to make sure the sentences are in order. Instruct the students to glue the sentences on the construction paper in order. *It is a good idea to keep the glue out of reach until you are sure that the words are correctly placed.* Assist where needed.

5. Give students an opportunity to read their sentences aloud.

Wednesday

Theme Time

See Monday for instructions on how to present the chapter, conduct a retelling, and teach vocabulary.

Potato Print Pictures

The purpose of this lesson is to provide a fun, theme-related art lesson. In addition, the word *potato* is reemphasized, and language skills are practiced.

Materials

- Potatoes
- Knife
- Tempera paint
- Newspaper
- Large sheets of construction paper

Instructions

1. Prepare the materials by carving designs into the cut end of potato halves.
2. Prepare a model.
3. Place materials in the center of the table.
4. Give students instructions and show the model.
5. Assist students when necessary.

Thursday

Ms. Jan's Group

Today, our counselor will be presenting a theme-related lesson on money. This is one example of how different team members relate their instruction to the overall theme.

She will teach skills such the importance of using money wisely and knowing how to count and use money for purchases.

Self-Selected Reading

See the self-selected reading plans for Monday.

Calendar and Writing Skills

Today's lesson will be used to teach social skills, calendar skills, and written expression skills.

Calendar Skills

1. Instruct students to take out their individual calendars.
2. Connect to prior learning by reminding students that the presentations are coming up and that an invitation is needed.
3. Through questioning, lead the students into locating the dates on which presentations are to be given.
4. Talk about the fact that we are inviting families to come see the presentations and that we need to write an invitation.

Writing an Invitation

The students will participate in the writing of the invitation. Because not all students are able to verbalize what they would like to say and because this is a fairly new skill, a set of words and Boardmaker symbols will be available on a magnetic white board. The symbols will be representative of things that one might commonly say in an invitation.

Other materials needed are a large piece of chart paper, clear tape, and a felt tip marker.

1. Go over the symbols that are displayed and explain what they mean.

2. Go over the words and read them with the students.

3. Explain that the students may use their own words or words from the communication notebooks or choose words or symbols displayed on the white board.

4. Choose a student who is most likely to understand instructions to be the first to tell you something that he would like to say in the invitation.

5. Either write or assist the student in writing the words on the chart paper. If the student chooses a word or symbol from the white board, then help the student use clear tape to attach the word or picture to the chart paper.

6. Continue until all students have had an opportunity to add words, phrases, or pictures to the chart.

7. Conclude the lesson by telling the students that on Friday you will all work together to write an invitation using their ideas.

One-on-One Instruction or Center Time

Practicing Presentations

1. Instruct students to either work on independent work or go to an assigned center.

2. All staff members will work with the same students whom they worked with on Monday to practice reading the presentations. If a student is using a PowerPoint presentation or a voice output device for the presentation, this will be practiced as well.

Guided Reading

Continue with practicing the reading of the presentations.

Friday

Self-Selected Reading

See the self-selected reading plans for Monday.

Theme Time

Writing Mini Lesson: Invitation

The teacher will model writing an invitation. On Thursday, the students participated in a brainstorming session by selecting words and phrases that they thought should be in the invitation. Today, these will be shaped into an invitation.

Materials

- A large chart page with an already written invitation for another event to be used as a model
- The chart page generated in Thursday's brainstorming session
- A new chart page
- Marker

Instructions

1. Connect to prior learning by reviewing the words and thoughts on the brainstorming chart, and discuss the need for an invitation.

2. Read and explain the model invitation to the students.
   - Think out loud, and write an invitation using the words and phrases from the brainstorming session.

3. Constantly refer to the model to find out what is needed in an invitation, and make this a part of your thinking out loud.
   - Example: "I see that this invitation says, 'You are invited.' Do we have that on our chart of ideas? Yes, here it is. I will write that up here because we want our families and friends to know that they are invited."

4. Encourage students to interact as you write by helping you find the words or phrases needed from the chart of ideas.
   - Ask them questions such as, "What do you think?" or, "Does that sound okay?"

5. Think out loud as you edit the invitation.

Follow Up

1. Type or hand-write the invitation over neatly on a nice piece of paper and make copies.

2. Teach the students how to sign the invitations and address envelopes.

Theme Time

Social Studies Lesson

One of the main characters in the book *Stone Fox* (Gardiner, 2003) is a Native American named Stone Fox. Today's lesson will provide an opportunity for students to learn about the Native American custom of choosing a name with a special meaning for a new baby. The lesson will also help them understand the name Stone Fox and its relationship to his character traits. Before beginning this lesson, the teacher will need to go to the Internet and find Native American names and their meanings. We used names used by the Cherokee people because they are our neighbors here in Western North Carolina.

Materials

- A magnetic white board or other display surface
- A selection of Cherokee (or other Native American) names typed and cut apart so that each name is separate and displayed on a white board
- The meaning of each name also cut apart and available, but not displayed, for matching to the name

Instructions

1. Connect this lesson to the prior learning by discussing the character Stone Fox and his name.
2. Explain that names sometimes match the traits of a person.
3. Explain that students will choose their own Native American name.
4. Read all names aloud.
5. Invite a student to come to the display area and choose a name.
6. Match the meaning of the name to the name and read it aloud, or allow the student to read it aloud.
7. Continue until all students have chosen a name.
8. Conclude by talking once more about the name Stone Fox and relating it to the traits of the character.
9. Connect the movie *Brother Bear* (Walt Disney, 2003) to prior learning by talking about the name Brother Bear and the fact that the story is about Native American People.
10. Show the movie *Brother Bear*.

Thematic Unit Planning Sheet

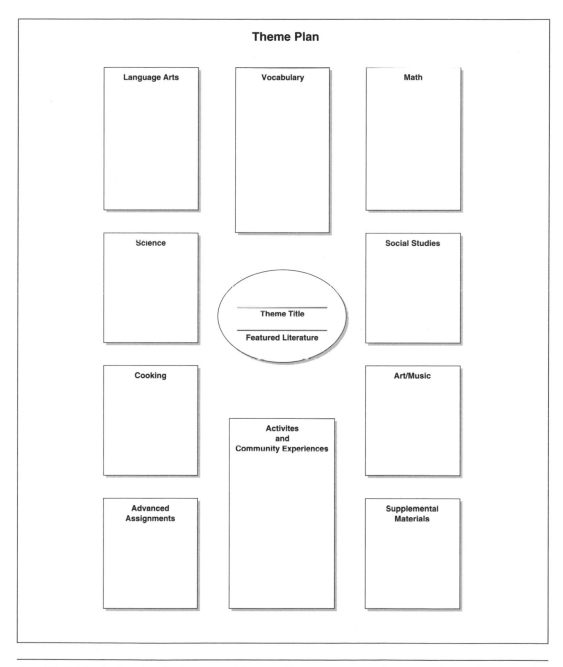

Theme Plan

Language Arts

Vocabulary

Math

Science

Social Studies

Theme Title

Featured Literature

Cooking

Art/Music

Activites
and
Community Experiences

Advanced
Assignments

Supplemental
Materials

Standard Course of Study Planning Sheet

Subject _____

Activity/Goal:

Course of Study Links

Materials	Plan/Notes

THE BLACK STALLION LESSON PLAN

COMPONENTS

Summary of *The Black Stallion* by Walter Farley

Theme Plan

Jungle Mural

Nonstandard Measurement and Estimation

Tornado in a Bottle

Group Teaching: Weather

Vocabulary

Bingo Samples

Sample IntelliTools Classroom Suite Activity Page

Summary of The Black Stallion *by Walter Farley*

Alec is a young boy who is traveling the world with his father. While on a ship returning to the United States, Alec discovers a beautiful Arabian stallion in the cargo area and becomes fascinated with this horse. The ship tragically sinks during a storm and the boy and horse are the only survivors and become stranded on an island. Alec and the horse are wary of each other at first, but eventually learn to trust each other, and develop a friendship as they ride around the island. A ship comes to rescue Alec, but the boy won't leave the island without the horse. Alec and the horse finally return to his hometown, but his mother is concerned with what to do with this magnificent but difficult animal. Alec meets Henry Daily, an elderly horse trainer living in his neighborhood. Henry realizes that Alec and Black have a special relationship, and together they begin to train the horse to race in championship races against the fastest horses in the area.

Theme Plan

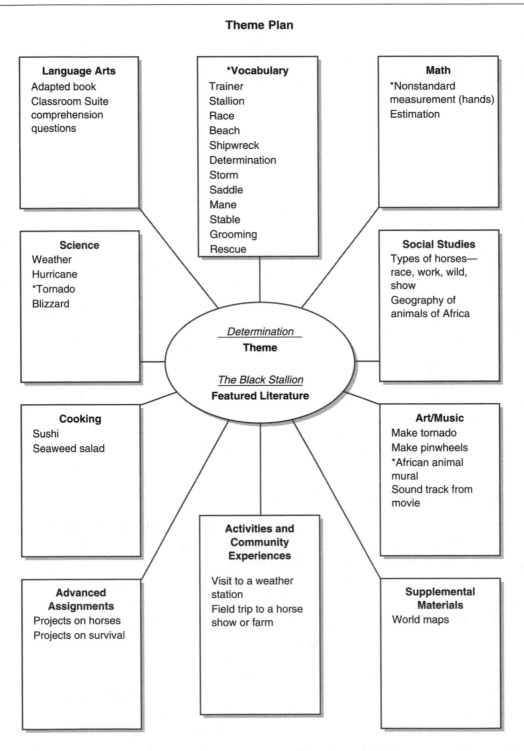

Theme Plan

Language Arts
Adapted book
Classroom Suite
comprehension
questions

*Vocabulary
Trainer
Stallion
Race
Beach
Shipwreck
Determination
Storm
Saddle
Mane
Stable
Grooming
Rescue

Math
*Nonstandard
measurement (hands)
Estimation

Science
Weather
Hurricane
*Tornado
Blizzard

Social Studies
Types of horses—
race, work, wild,
show
Geography of
animals of Africa

Determination
Theme

The Black Stallion
Featured Literature

Cooking
Sushi
Seaweed salad

Art/Music
Make tornado
Make pinwheels
*African animal
mural
Sound track from
movie

**Advanced
Assignments**
Projects on horses
Projects on survival

**Activities and
Community
Experiences**

Visit to a weather
station
Field trip to a horse
show or farm

**Supplemental
Materials**
World maps

Jungle Mural

Students will develop fine motor skills, learn about animals of Africa, and have fun as they help make a large jungle mural

Materials

- Paint rollers in a variety of sizes
- Large sheet of white and brown paper (the type used for a bulletin board backgrounds)
- Styrofoam plates or trays
- Large sheets of construction paper
  - Green
  - Brown
  - Gray
  - Black
  - Yellow
  - Orange
  - Brown
  - Red
- Paint
  - Yellow
  - Green
  - Brown

Instructions

1. Cut a large sheet of white paper for a mural background.
2. Mix different shades of green paint using the yellow and green and pour onto the Styrofoam plates.
3. Invite the students to cover the white paper with different shades of green paint using the rollers.
4. Allow the background to dry.
5. Cut long strips of brown paper about 6 to 12 inches wide.
6. Invite the students to help twist the paper to make long vines.
7. Draw tropical leaf shapes on the large green construction paper and invite the students to help cut out the leaves.
8. Invite the students to help make textures on the leaves using the rollers and the shades of green paint.
9. Work with the students to make large cutouts of jungle animals, flowers, birds and butterflies.
10. Glue the leaves, vines, birds, animals, and flowers onto the background to create a jungle mural.

Nonstandard Measurement and Estimation

In this activity, students will use nonstandard measurements to measure things around the classroom. The students enjoy comparing their measurements to others'. It is also fun to get staff involved to see the differences in hand and feet size for the entire classroom.

Materials

- Instruments of measure: ruler, yardstick, measuring tape, measuring cup, liquid measuring cup, thermometer, and so on
- Construction or bulletin board paper in all different colors
- Pencils for tracing
- Scissors
- Chart paper
- White board
- Tape

Instructions

1. Instruct students to choose a paper color.
2. Assist (if needed) in tracing students' hands.
3. Assist (if needed) cutting out the traced hands.
4. Write students' names on the back of the cut out hands.
5. Gather cut out hands.
6. Discuss different ways to measure using the different measuring tools
7. Instruct the class that they are going to learn to measure using "our class" measurement.
8. Have everyone show their hands and discuss how different the sizes are.
9. Choose different items in the room to measure such as a table, a desk, a closet, the door frame, and so on.
10. Ask students to look at their hands and look at the item to be measured. Ask, "How many hands high (or long) do you think this (table) is?" Write the estimations on the white board. Discuss the definition of *estimation*.
11. Measure items using the cut out hands, taping each hand down. As you tape down the hand, ask the class to count aloud with you.

For example, if you are measuring a table, place a hand down, tape it, say "One," place another hand down (wrist to middle finger) and say "two," and continue until the measurement is complete.

12. When the measurement is complete, count aloud again the number of hands used.

13. Look at the estimations. Make statements such as, "Jennifer said she thought it would take 12 hands to measure the table. When we counted, we found it took 15 hands to measure the table. Was Jennifer's estimation or guess higher or lower?"

14. Continue the measurements until it is complete.

15. Choose the largest hand and the smallest hand in the classroom.

16. Measure the longest item in the classroom (a door frame is a good visual item).

17. Show the class the largest hand in the classroom and ask for estimations of the item's measurement.

18. Follow directions 12–14.

19. Repeat 18 and 19 using the smallest hand in the classroom.

20. Discuss the differences in measurements and ask questions such as, "If it is very important to be correct in a measurement, would you use a ruler or the 'our class' measurement?"

Tornado in a Bottle

Students will enjoy working as a group to make a tornado. This lesson provides an opportunity for guided reading as well as a math lesson. This lesson should follow a lesson in which students learn about tornadoes.

Materials

- A plastic bottle such as a two-liter drink bottle with cap
- Measuring spoons
- A tiny house such as the ones found in Monopoly
- Salt
- Dishwashing liquid
- Blue food coloring
- Ruler
- Marker

Preparation

Write the following directions on a chart. If you have students who are emergent readers, you may want to include symbols on your chart.

1. Use a ruler and measure one inch from the top of the bottle. Mark the one-inch line with a marker.
2. Fill the bottle with water up to the mark.
3. Measure one teaspoon of salt and pour it into the bottle.
4. Place the cap on the bottle.
5. Shake the bottle until the salt is dissolved.
6. Take off the cap and add the dishwashing liquid and the food coloring.
7. Put the house in the bottle.
8. Cover the bottle.
9. Move the bottle around and around making the water swirl.
10. Watch and see what happens.

Instructions

1. Review tornado facts.
2. Place the materials on a table.
3. Have the students help read the steps on the chart.
4. Invite students to take turns following the steps.
5. Talk about the results with the students, explaining how the tornado in the bottle is like a real tornado.

Group Teaching: Weather

Most of the classrooms in our program are in one wing of our school. We have five classrooms and teachers. When all of the classrooms participate in a theme, (usually two or three times a year) we divide a particular lesson into five parts. Students rotate between classes to learn parts of the lesson. This has turned out to be one of the favorite parts of the themes for the students. They get to leave the classroom (with teacher assistants) and visit other classrooms and have access to teachers they see every day in the hallway. Each teacher has a different style of teaching, so the students get to be involved in a variety of teaching methods.

For *The Black Stallion*, we decided there were two areas that were conducive to this type of teaching. The first subject was "weather." Each teacher chose a particular part of weather she was interested in, and we set up a time a few weeks ahead for the lessons to take place. We did *hurricane, tornado, blizzard, thunderstorm,* and *drought*. We found some amazing Web sites and lesson plans for teaching this subject, and the students thoroughly enjoyed it.

The second area was "different types of horses." We used show horses, workhorses, horses in the rodeo, racehorses, and wild horses. Again, there were many good Web sites to use for developing lesson plans. One of the teacher's parents had a farm, and the teacher brought in a saddle and grooming tools. Students were able to sit on the saddle and get a hands-on feel for tools needed to groom a horse.

There are several reasons that group teaching is beneficial. The first one is that it makes teaching easier! You just have to develop one lesson plan for five (or however many teachers you are working with) classes. As stated before, the students get to learn with different teaching styles. Because we were working with different student populations, it also challenged our teachers to figure out ways to reach different types of students. It also helped with team building among our teachers and helped us get a different view of the students and teachers in our program.

Vocabulary

trainer

beach

shipwreck

stormy

race

stallion

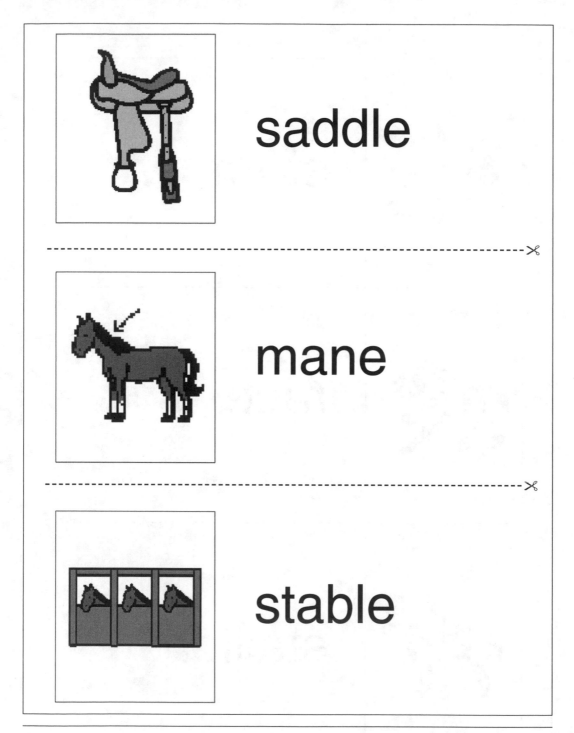

saddle

mane

stable

rescue

grooming

determinatior

Communication Board

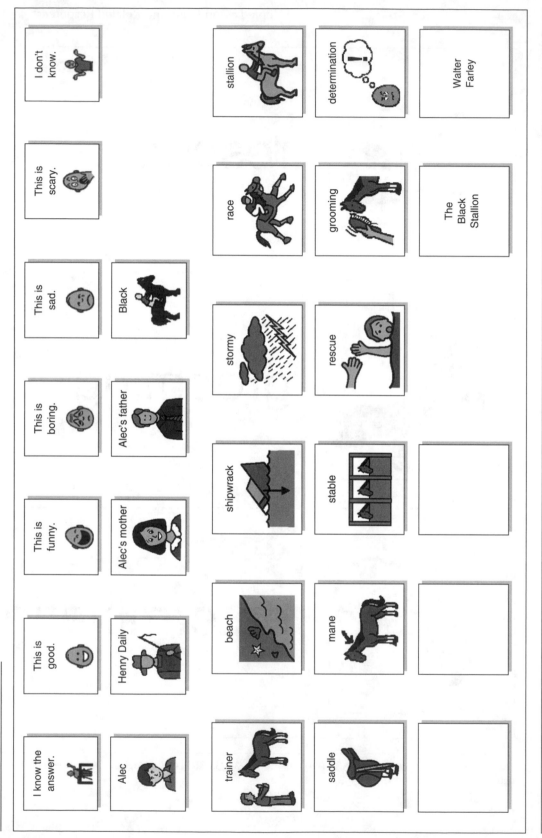

I know the answer.	This is good.	This is funny.	This is boring.	This is sad.	This is scary.	I don't know.
Alec	Henry Daily	Alec's mother	Alec's father	Black		

trainer	beach	shipwrack	stormy		race	stallion
saddle	mane	stable	rescue	grooming	determination	
				The Black Stallion	Walter Farley	

Bingo Samples

Sample IntelliTools Classroom Suite Activity Page

Classroom Suite - [Black Stallion (IntelliTalk 3)]

File   Edit   Text   View   Options   IntelliTalk   Window   Help

read text

The Black Stallion

1. Someone who teaches a person or animal to do something is a _____.

2. A sandy place next to the ocean is called a _____.

3. When it rains, thunders and has lots of lightening, it is called a _____.

4. A terrible storm on the ocean caused a _____.

5. When you save someone from danger it is called a _____.

6. A boy horse is called a _____.

7. When Alec rode Black, he sat on a _____.

8. The hair on the horse's neck is the _____.

9. Black live in a _____.

10. Brushing a horse's coat and combing the mane is called _____

11. At the end of the book, Alec and Black won the _____.

12. To try very, very hard is to have _____.

print

determination   grooming

trainer   rescue

beach   stable

mane   storm

shipwreck   race

stallion   saddle

ISLAND OF THE BLUE DOLPHINS LESSON PLAN

COMPONENTS

Summary of *Island of the Blue Dolphins* by Scott O'Dell

Theme Plan

Make an Island

Student Presentations

Sample Parent Letter

Sand Casting

Vocabulary

Communication Board

Parent Letter

Summary of Island of the Blue Dolphins *by Scott O'Dell*

Karana is growing up on an island in the Pacific Ocean. The people in her village supply food to their tribe by picking roots and fishing in the shallow waters around the island. A group of Aleuts come to the island looking for otters and try to leave without paying for them. A fight breaks out, and many people on both sides are killed. Later, an elder tribe member leaves the island and sends a ship back to rescue the remaining people. A storm approaches as the ship is preparing to leave. Karana realizes that her brother, Ramo, has been left behind, and she jumps in the water and swims to shore as the boat sails away. Ramo is tragically killed by a pack of wild dogs, and Karana must now live alone on the island. After killing many of the wild dogs in anger, Karana befriends one and names him Rontu because of his yellow eyes. Karana and Rontu are marooned for many years on the island. During that time she gathers food, makes her clothes, and creates a home in a secluded cave and stocks it with food.

Karana is constantly watching for the Aleuts to return to the island. One day their ships land on the shore, and Karana and Rontu hide in the cave. Despite her efforts to stay hidden, Karana meets one of the young women from the ship and realizes how lonely she has become. The Aleuts finally leave the island, and Karana and the animals return to their daily routines.

Rontu eventually dies, and Karana adopts one of his puppies, names him Rontu Aru, and brings him to the cave to live with her. After many years, a rescue ship arrives to take Karana off of the island. She leaves with Rontu Aru and returns to live in the mission on the coast of California at Santa Barbara.

This book is based on a real woman named Juana Maria, who was rescued from the island in 1853 and died seven weeks after returning to the mainland.

Theme Plan

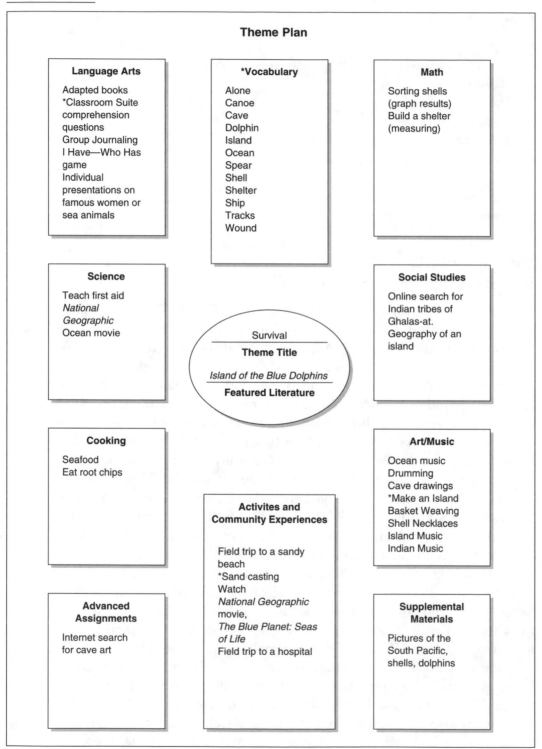

Theme Plan

Language Arts

Adapted books
*Classroom Suite
comprehension
questions
Group Journaling
I Have—Who Has
game
Individual
presentations on
famous women or
sea animals

*Vocabulary

Alone
Canoe
Cave
Dolphin
Island
Ocean
Spear
Shell
Shelter
Ship
Tracks
Wound

Math

Sorting shells
(graph results)
Build a shelter
(measuring)

Science

Teach first aid
*National
Geographic*
Ocean movie

Survival
Theme Title

Island of the Blue Dolphins
Featured Literature

Social Studies

Online search for
Indian tribes of
Ghalas-at.
Geography of an
island

Cooking

Seafood
Eat root chips

**Activites and
Community Experiences**

Field trip to a sandy
beach
*Sand casting
Watch
National Geographic
movie,
*The Blue Planet: Seas
of Life*
Field trip to a hospital

Art/Music

Ocean music
Drumming
Cave drawings
*Make an Island
Basket Weaving
Shell Necklaces
Island Music
Indian Music

**Advanced
Assignments**

Internet search
for cave art

**Supplemental
Materials**

Pictures of the
South Pacific,
shells, dolphins

Make an Island

Students will learn about how an island is formed in this activity. You can add as much scientific detail as you want to explore how islands are made, or use it as an art activity.

Materials

- 12" × 12" sheets of cardboard
- Blue modeling compound or clay—enough to cover cardboard
- White modeling compound or clay—smaller portion than blue
- Brown modeling compound or clay—smaller portion than white
- Sand
- Items to decorate island and ocean:
  o Plastic palm trees
  o Grass
  o Plastic shrubbery
  o Small rocks
  o Small seashells
  o Sea creatures
  o Beach creatures

Instructions

1. Distribute a sheet of cardboard to each student.

2. Distribute blue modeling compound or clay to each student.

3. Instruct student to press out modeling compound or clay to cover the entire cardboard area, about $\frac{1}{8}$" thick. Demonstrate how thumb imprints look like waves.

4. Distribute white modeling compound or clay.

5. Ask students where they would like their island and have them put the white modeling compound or clay in that space. Press flat to about $\frac{1}{2}$" thick.

6. Distribute brown modeling compound or clay.

7. Ask students where they would like their land to be on the island and put the brown modeling compound or clay in that space.

8. Demonstrate how to shape mountain areas as well as flatter areas on the white modeling compound or clay.

9. Place sand on top of white modeling compound or clay, pressing it in slightly. Decorate the sand with beach creatures.

10. Decorate brown modeling compound or clay with grass, plastic trees, and other items.

11. Decorate blue modeling compound or clay with sea creatures.

Student Presentations

In our classroom, as in general education, presentations provide opportunities for the students to share information on a topic of their choice. Students learn about their topic, then use their own voice or communication devices to teach the other students in the classroom.

Materials

- Communication Devices
- IntelliTools program
- Computer program that reads text aloud
- Microphone or karaoke machine
- Pointer
- Stand
- Poster holder (such as a chart stand)

We have found that the student-presentations part of our thematic units has been a favorite activity for the students and staff. It is also an opportunity for the students to work with their parents. Watching our students give a report just like any other middle-school student is a very meaningful experience. We do not include student presentations with every unit because we want to keep it exciting for the students and parents. As in any middle-school classroom, there are students whose parents do not work with them on a project or presentation, so classroom staff works with those students to complete the projects.

We have done the actual presentations a couple of different ways. In the classroom, we set up an area in the front of the room with all the equipment needed for each student. Students came to the front with the teacher or an assistant and presented a topic. For a change of scenery, we have also reserved the library, which makes the presentations seem a little more formal. During some of the presentations, we have invited administrators and other school personnel.

Sample Parent Letter

One of our first student-presentation opportunities was during the theme "Survival," using the book *Island of the Blue Dolphins.* A copy of our parent letter, which helps explain the presentations and gives examples of topics, appears on the next page.

Another way we have chosen projects is to get a picture of each of the topic items and put them on a chart. Each student comes to the board and chooses the topic of his or her choice by placing his or her name under the picture. We decided it was fine for duplicate topics to be covered because each student does a report differently. This also helps with students whose parents and guardians are not able to help so staff can begin working with them.

Dear Parents/Guardians,

On our schedule for next week, we will begin discussing reports on special topics we have chosen for our "Survival" theme to go along with our book *Island of the Blue Dolphins*. The students will be presenting their reports at the end of our unit. Over the next few days, please have a discussion with your child and decide what he or she (and you!) would like to work on. We have chosen the topic of ocean animals because the setting of the book is an island in the Pacific Ocean and "Famous Women" because Karana, in the story, is so strong and resourceful.

These are the suggested topics:

Ocean Animals	Famous Women
Dolphin	Clara Barton
Whale	Amelia Earhart
Stingray	Betsy Ross
Clam	Joan of Arc
Otter	Ethel Kennedy
Seal	Mother Theresa
Crab	Madame Curie
Clown Fish	Florence Nightingale
Shark	Harriet Tubman

If you or your child think of another sea creature or famous woman for a presentation, please feel free to make another choice. Complete the form on the next page and send it in on Tuesday.

We would like the reports to be as visual as possible, with lots of pictures. It does not have to be long. You and your child can use a poster, a book, or any type of format you like. If your child is not verbal, we will help with communication devices so he or she can present the material. If you are not able to help with the report, please let us know, and we will work with your child. After the report is finished, please review the highlights so your child will be more comfortable with the presentation.

Let us know if you have any questions!

Dotty and Jill

I, _____, would like to do my report on _____.
   student name   topic

_____
parent/guardian signature

_____ I would like my child to work with classroom staff on this project.

Sand Casting

This craft activity provides a lot of enjoyment along with the opportunity for guided reading instruction. Learning to follow directions and planning will occur in a natural, fun way. We were able to take a trip to a lake and make the sand castings directly in the sand along the shore. If you are unable to be on a beach, placing the sand in a shallow container in the classroom will provide a good alternative.

Materials

- Sand
- Plaster of paris
- Shells
- Plastic or polystyrene trays or other shallow containers (only if you must do this activity in the classroom)
- Step-by-step instructions using a large chart, symbols, written words, or both (or, if on the beach, use printed instructions on a letter-size piece of paper)
- Water
- Large spoon
- Small plastic buckets or coffee cans for mixing
- Communication devices with related vocabulary available

Preparation

Print steps in simple language on a large chart or make individual copies on letter-size paper. Use symbols when needed. The steps to be printed are these:

Steps

1. Scoop out some sand to make a shape that you would like. Some people make circles, some make a fish shape, some make a shape like a jellyfish. This hole in the sand should be about as deep as your thumb and about the size of a grownup person's hand.
2. Place shells or other decorations such as twigs in the bottom of the hole.
3. Mix the plaster in a coffee can or other container, following the instructions.
4. Pour the plaster over the entire arrangement, filling the hole.
5. Let the plaster dry completely.
6. Once the plaster is completely dry, gently pull your beautiful piece of work out of the sand.

Make a model by following the instructions in the next section.

Instructions

1. If on the beach, divide the students into small groups paired with an adult. If the students are in the classroom, it may work best to go through the steps as a group.

2. Begin by showing the students the model and going over the instructions.

3. Return to the beginning of the instructions and have students volunteer to help by reading each step. As each step is read, each student or small group will complete the step before the group moves to the next step.

Vocabulary

island

- ✂

ocean

- ✂

shells

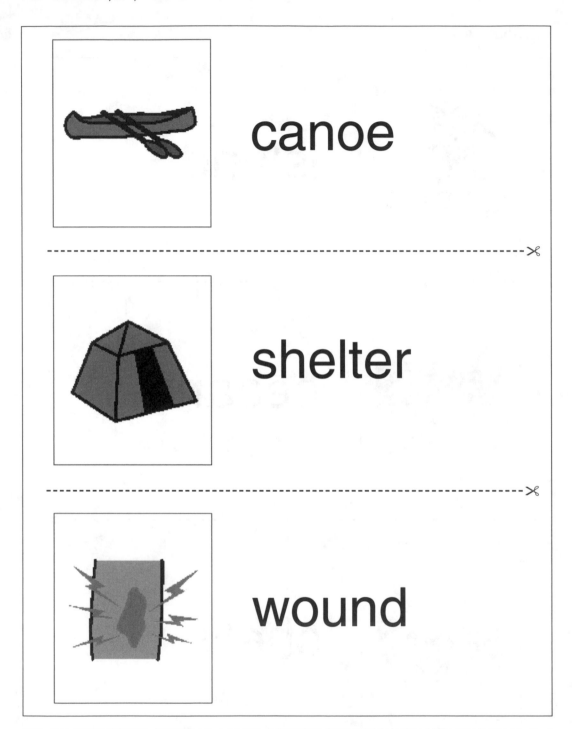

canoe

shelter

wound

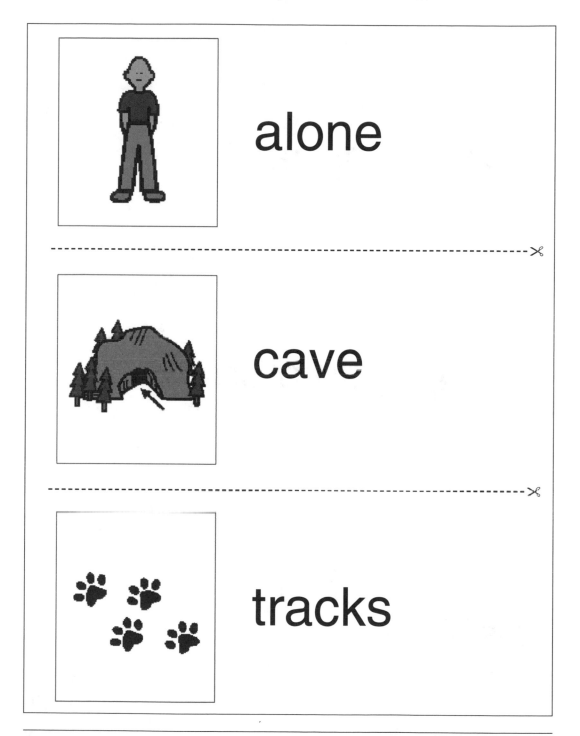

alone

cave

tracks

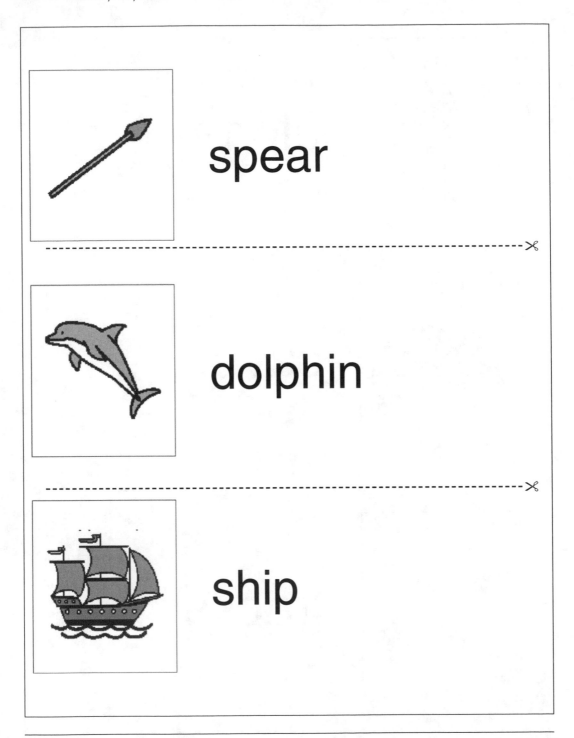

spear

dolphin

ship

Communication Board

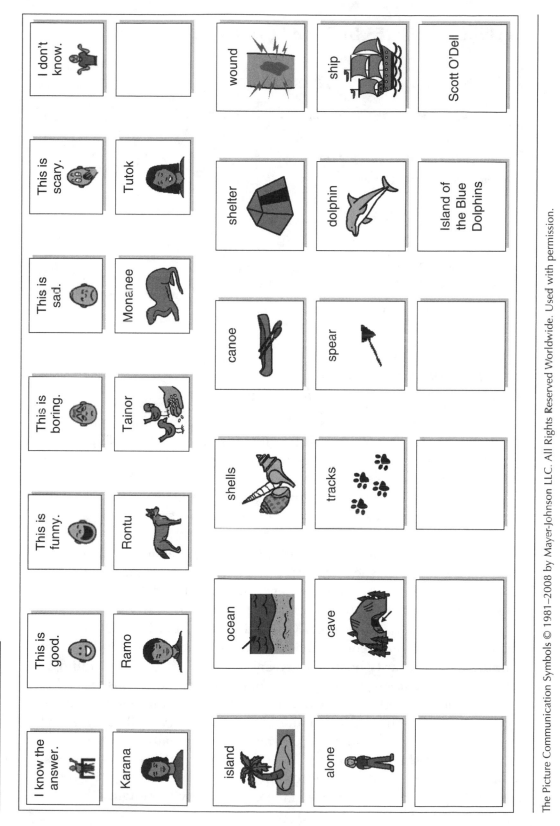

I know the answer.	This is good.	This is funny.	This is boring.	This is sad.	This is scary.	I don't know.
Karana	Ramo	Rontu	Tainor	Monanee	Tutok	

island	ocean	shells	canoe	shelter	wound
alone	cave	tracks	spear	dolphin	ship
				Island of the Blue Dolphins	Scott O'Dell

WHERE THE LILIES BLOOM LESSON PLAN

COMPONENTS

Summary of *Where the Lilies Bloom* by Vera and Bill Cleaver

Theme Plan

Family Tree: Social Studies Activity

Mountain Views: Art Activity

Quilt Day

Stone Soup and Trip to the Farmers' Market

Field Trip

Making Stone Soup

Vocabulary

Communication Board

Summary of Where the Lilies Bloom *by Vera and Bill Cleaver*

Where the Lilies Bloom is a moving story of the struggles of life in the rural Appalachian Mountains. Mary Call Luther is a fourteen-year-old girl who struggles to keep her family together after the death of both of their parents. Mary Call lives with an eighteen-year-old sister, Devola, a ten-year-old brother, Romey, and a five-year-old sister, Ima Dean. As their father lay dying, he made Mary Call promise to do several things. First, she must always take pride in the Luther name and teach her siblings to do likewise. Second, she must keep the family together and refuse charity after his death. Third, she must not call a preacher or undertaker when he dies. Fourth, she must never allow Devola to marry Kiser Pease, who owns the land that the Luthers have been sharecropping for him.

When Roy Luther dies, Mary Call and Romey bury him but keep his death a secret to prevent neighbors from separating the children and putting them in charity homes. Mary Call finds a book on "wildcrafting," and the family starts using the plant resources in the mountains to combat their extreme poverty. An extremely harsh winter pushes the Luther children to their physical and emotional limits. Mary Call realizes that Kiser Pease really does love Devola, and she eventually allows them to marry. With the help of Kiser and Devola, the three other children remain in the Luther home and continue to earn money by wildcrafting. This book gives a fascinating picture of life in the Great Smoky Mountains.

Theme Plan

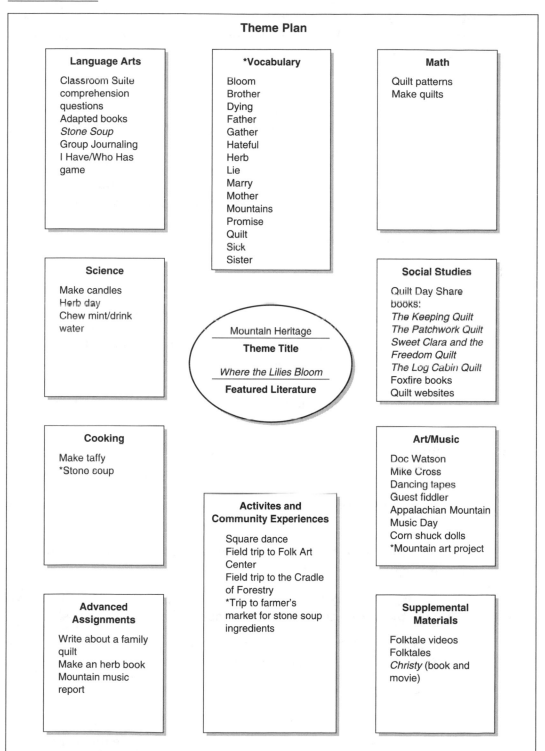

Theme Plan

Language Arts

Classroom Suite comprehension questions
Adapted books
Stone Soup
Group Journaling
I Have/Who Has game

*Vocabulary

Bloom
Brother
Dying
Father
Gather
Hateful
Herb
Lie
Marry
Mother
Mountains
Promise
Quilt
Sick
Sister

Math

Quilt patterns
Make quilts

Science

Make candles
Herb day
Chew mint/drink water

Mountain Heritage
Theme Title
Where the Lilies Bloom
Featured Literature

Social Studies

Quilt Day Share books:
The Keeping Quilt
The Patchwork Quilt
Sweet Clara and the Freedom Quilt
The Log Cabin Quilt
Foxfire books
Quilt websites

Cooking

Make taffy
*Stone soup

Art/Music

Doc Watson
Mike Cross
Dancing tapes
Guest fiddler
Appalachian Mountain Music Day
Corn shuck dolls
*Mountain art project

Activites and Community Experiences

Square dance
Field trip to Folk Art Center
Field trip to the Cradle of Forestry
*Trip to farmer's market for stone soup ingredients

Advanced Assignments

Write about a family quilt
Make an herb book
Mountain music report

Supplemental Materials

Folktale videos
Folktales
Christy (book and movie)

Family Tree: Social Studies Activity

As the students talk about the characters in *Where the Lilies Bloom,* they will learn about family roles and better understand the roles of their own family members.

Materials

- A large sheet of brown art paper (the kind that is used for a bulletin board background)
- Blank sentence strips
- Boardmaker symbols representing sister, father, brother, and mother paired with the words (provided on the communication pages with this unit)
- Pictures representing the characters

Preparation

1. Use the sheet of brown paper to make a large tree.

2. Write the words *father, mother, sister,* and *brother* on sentence strips.

3. Put the large tree up on a wall.

4. Have the symbols of family members and characters cut out and ready.

Instructions

1. Seat the students in a group in front of the tree.

2. Give the symbols that represent family members to the students who are learning to recognize pictures.

3. Give the words written on the sentence strips to the students who are beginning to read.

4. Talk about family roles (sister, brother, etc.). Determine prior knowledge by questioning the students about their own families.

5. Present a picture of a character, and talk about the character's role in the family in *Where the Lilies Bloom.*

6. Place the picture on the tree.

7. Ask, " Who has the word _____?"

8. Once the word is identified, have the student place the word beside the picture of the character.

9. Ask, "Who has the picture of _____?"

10. Proceed in this manner until all members of Mary Call's family have been placed on the family tree.

Mountain Views: Art Activity

This art activity will result in one-of-a-kind mountain landscapes in shades of blue and purple. The students will have fun as they use communication systems to request materials and to comment. They will have a sense of accomplishment as they learn that they can produce a pretty product to show off to friends and family.

Materials

- Construction paper in shades of blue and purple
- White construction paper (12" × 18" sheets)
- School glue
- Black and white tempera paint
- Foam paint rollers
- Natural sea sponges
- Shallow containers

Preparation

1. Work with the students to tear the blue and purple construction paper into pieces roughly the size of small index cards. Tear some into rough triangle shapes to form the peaks of the mountains.

2. Mix white and black paint to form shades of gray for the sky.

3. Place the different shades of gray in shallow containers appropriate for using small sponge rollers.

4. Place the white paint in a shallow container.

5. Make a model for your students.

Instructions

1. Using the foam paint rollers, roll different shades of gray together to make a stormy sky. This should cover at least the top two thirds of your paper.

2. Sponge in white clouds using the natural sea sponges. Allow the paint to dry.

3. Begin putting in mountains by gluing the lightest shades of blue and purple about one third of the way down the page, forming mountain peaks. Continue to make rows of mountains using darker shades of torn paper. The mountains closest to the bottom or the page should be the darkest shades of blue and purple. When you view the Appalachian Mountains in the distance, the lightest colors seen are in the distance, and the darkest colors are close.

Tip

After the pictures dry, stack them under heavy books or magazines overnight to assure that they will be smooth.

Quilt Day

This is an activity that involves the students and their families. Students learn about family history and how to present that information to the classroom.

Preparation

1. In your parent letter at the beginning of the theme, include a note home to parents or guardians to send in a special quilt.

2. Ask them to write a note about the quilt and how it is special to the family.

3. Ask that all quilts be sent in on a specified day.

Instructions

1. On "Quilt Day," students and staff can share information about their favorite quilt.

2 Some children may need assistance with reading the notes sent in, and others can use augmentative communication.

3. Following is a sample note.

Dear Parents/Guardians,

In *Where the Lilies Bloom,* quilts play an important part in the family's daily life. On
_____, we will be having a "Quilt Day," and we would like to learn more about
your family quilts. Please send in your special quilt (we will take care of it!) and a
note explaining why it is special to your child and to your family. Here are some
things we would be interested in learning about the quilt: How old is the quilt? Did
it originally belong to someone else? Did someone you know make the quilt? Is
there special material in the quilt? Do you know what type of design it is or what
it means? Does it stay in a special place in your home? Did you or your child sleep
with it as a baby, or do one of you use it now? Any other information you know
about the quilt will be helpful.

   We will assist your child as needed in telling the class about the quilt. We will
use your child's communication device or other technology to help your child tell
about your family quilt.

Thank you,

teacher name(s)

Stone Soup *and Trip to the Farmers' Market*

These activities are a fun way to incorporate reading and writing into a
cooking activity. The students will learn about brainstorming ideas, planning for cooking a recipe, shopping skills, and following a recipe.

Materials

- Chart paper
- Markers
- Boardmaker symbols of different types of vegetables

Instructions

1. Plan a field trip to the local farmer's market or supermarket.

2. Discuss what type of foods the family ate in *Where the Lilies Bloom,*
   especially the vegetables.

3. Using a chart, brainstorm items that might go into vegetable soup.
   List the choices on the chart paper. You can also ask students what
   their favorite vegetables are. For students who are nonverbal, use
   Boardmaker symbols.

4. Read *Stone Soup*. There are many versions of this story published in book form, so choose the one that has the best illustrations.

5. Point out vegetables in the story that students chose.

6. Choose your favorite vegetable soup recipe. Some of the *Stone Soup* books have recipes in them. Here is the one we used from the *More-With-Less Cookbook* (Longacre, 1976).

Timeless Vegetable-Beef Soup

1 large beef soup bone
2 qts. Water
$1\frac{1}{2}$ t. salt
$\frac{1}{4}$ t. pepper
1 bay leaf

   Combine ingredients in large pot. Cover and simmer 2–3 hours. Remove bones and skim fat. Cut off, chop, and reserve meat. Add:
2 large carrots
1 large potatoes
1 cup green beans
1 cup celery
$\frac{1}{2}$ cup onion
1 large shredded cabbage
2 cups cooked (or canned) tomatoes
herbs and seasonings to taste
reserved meat

   Cook until vegetables are tender.

7. Look at the list the students made. If there are any vegetables they chose, ask if they want them in the soup, too.

Field Trip

Materials

- Boardmaker symbols of ingredients in the soup
- Individual item from the recipe for each student—you can either make a copy of the recipe for each student and highlight the students' individual item or list them separately
- Pencils for marking

Instructions

1. Divide students into pairs (or groups, according to how large your class is).

2. Give each pair or group one item from the recipe. Try to give them their favorite one or one they chose for the list if possible.

3. Tell the students this is the item they are responsible for finding at the market.

4. Ask students where in the market or store they think the item might be found. Ask them to find their item, and assist them as needed. When the students find their item, have them put a check mark beside it on the list and return to a designated area.

5. Review the recipe with the group to make sure every item has been obtained.

6. Have students pay for their individual item if possible.

Making Stone Soup

Materials

- Chart paper
- Markers
- Items needed to make the soup

Instructions

1. Write the recipe in large letters on chart paper.

2. Review the recipe with the class.

3. Discuss what each student bought at the market.

4. Have students do individual jobs according to ability, such as cut carrots, add pepper, and so on. (We have student names in a box and draw names for each job).

5. Reread *Stone Soup* while the soup is cooking.

6. While eating the soup with your students, point out things such as, "I see the carrots Lacy found," or "I taste the pepper Anthony put in the soup."

Vocabulary

brother

promise

herb

quilt

bloom

sick

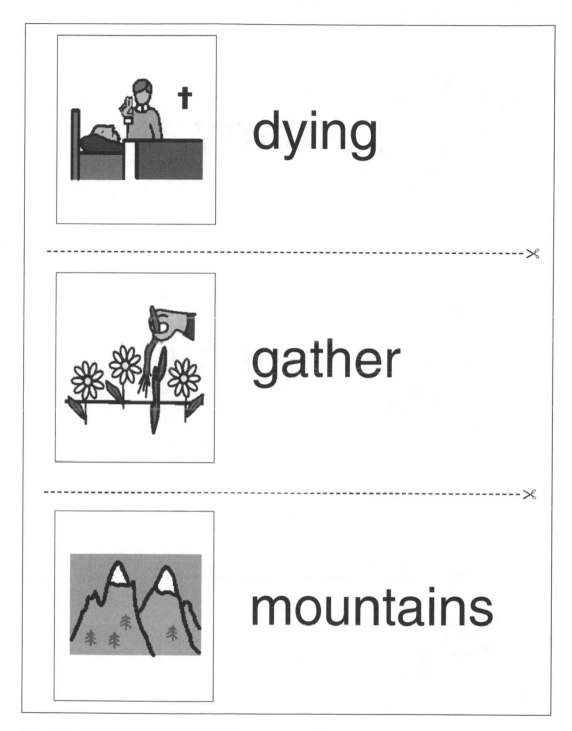

dying

gather

mountains

marry

hateful

lie

Communication Board

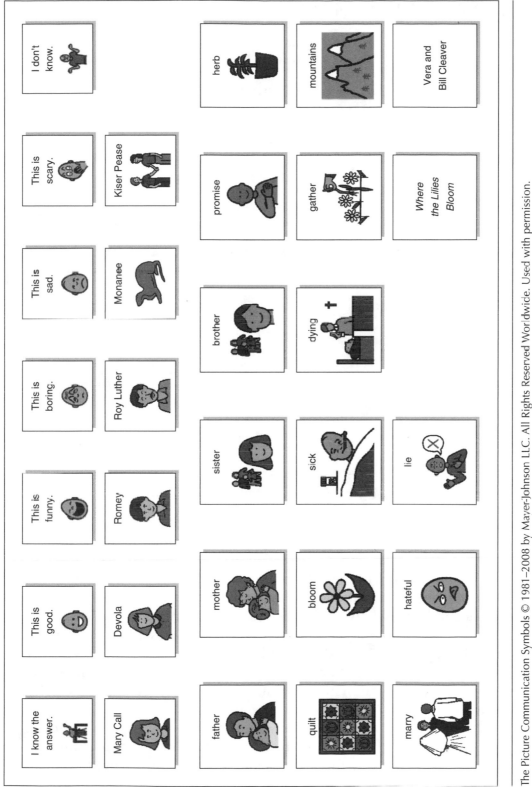

I know the answer.	This is good.	This is funny.	This is boring.	This is sad.	This is scary.	I don't know.

Mary Call	Devola	Romey	Roy Luther	Monanee	Kiser Pease

father	mother	sister	brother	promise	herb
quilt	bloom	sick	dying	gather	mountains
marry	hateful	lie		Where the Lilies Bloom	Vera and Bill Cleaver

STONE FOX LESSON PLAN

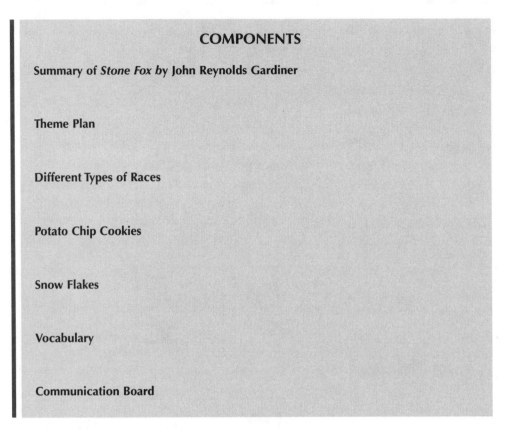

COMPONENTS

Summary of *Stone Fox* by John Reynolds Gardiner

Theme Plan

Different Types of Races

Potato Chip Cookies

Snow Flakes

Vocabulary

Communication Board

Summary of Stone Fox *by John Reynolds Gardiner*

Little Willy lives with his grandfather on a potato farm near Jackson, Wyoming. Willy's grandfather becomes ill and can't pay the land taxes and might lose this farm. Willy decides to enter his dog, Searchlight, in a dogsled race to win the $500 prize to pay the taxes. Also entered in the race is a Native American, Stone Fox, who drives a team of malamutes and inevitably wins the race each year. Stone Fox uses the prize money to buy back the land he feels that the white settlers have stolen from his people. Willy's dog Searchlight strives to keep up with the experienced team, and they race neck and neck for the finish line. The race offers a dramatic ending demonstrating respect and generosity between the rivals.

Note: In the book, the grandfather raises potatoes, but in the movie, he raises cattle. Although this book does provide an opportunity to compare and contrast, this may not be a theme you would want to teach first.

Theme Plan

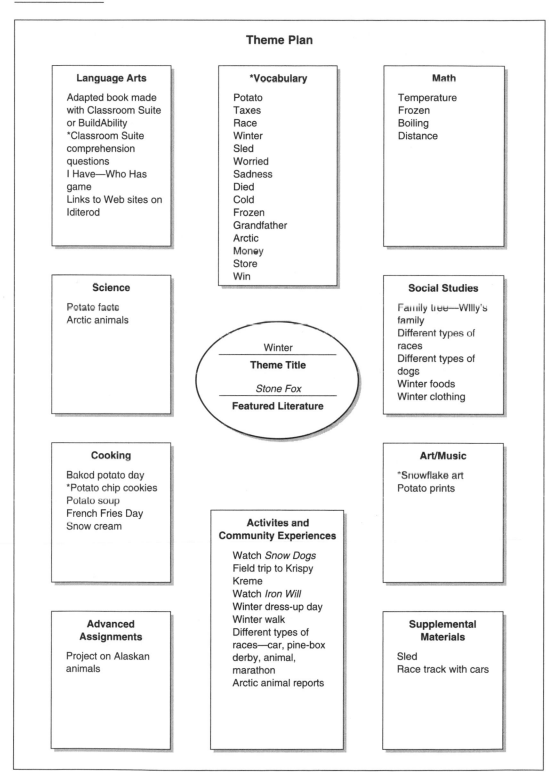

Theme Plan

Language Arts

Adapted book made with Classroom Suite or BuildAbility
*Classroom Suite comprehension questions
I Have—Who Has game
Links to Web sites on Iditerod

*Vocabulary

Potato
Taxes
Race
Winter
Sled
Worried
Sadness
Died
Cold
Frozen
Grandfather
Arctic
Money
Store
Win

Math

Temperature
Frozen
Boiling
Distance

Science

Potato facts
Arctic animals

Winter
Theme Title

Stone Fox
Featured Literature

Social Studies

Family tree—Willy's family
Different types of races
Different types of dogs
Winter foods
Winter clothing

Cooking

Baked potato day
*Potato chip cookies
Potato soup
French Fries Day
Snow cream

Art/Music

*Snowflake art
Potato prints

Activites and Community Experiences

Watch *Snow Dogs*
Field trip to Krispy Kreme
Watch *Iron Will*
Winter dress-up day
Winter walk
Different types of races—car, pine-box derby, animal, marathon
Arctic animal reports

Advanced Assignments

Project on Alaskan animals

Supplemental Materials

Sled
Race track with cars

Different Types of Races

In this lesson, students will learn about different types of races around the world through the use of technology. They will brainstorm ideas and then graph their favorite type of race.

Materials

- Data projector
- Chart paper
- Markers
- Names of each student
- Tape

Instructions

1. Using the chart paper and markers, ask students to name different types of races. You may want to discuss different car (did you know "racecar" spelled backwards is "racecar"?!) races or Olympic activities to get them going.

2. After brainstorming ideas, tell the students you are going to show them different types of races on the Internet.

3. Use a data projector to look at different types of races. Some helpful Web sites are

   www.wikipedia.org/wiki/Racing
   www.olympic.org/uk/utilities/multimedia/gallery/index_uk.asp
   There are many different Web sites that cover races involving running, cars, and animal races, such as dog and horse racing. Review the Web sites to assure they are appropriate. There are many "wacky racing" sites that are fun but may have some material not suitable for students.

4. After a review of the material on the Internet, ask students what their favorite race is.

5. List the races across the bottom of the chart paper.

6. Have the students rate their favorite race by drawing names from a box. Give each student an opportunity to come up to the chart paper and place their name above their favorite race.

7. Discuss the graph and determine the favorite race.

Potato Chip Cookies

When we were looking for activities using potatoes, we came across an interesting recipe using potato chips. It is an interesting cookie that is salty and sweet at the same time. Students will learn about different uses for an ingredient as well as measurement and sequencing events.

Materials

- Chart paper
- Markers
- Recipe for potato chip cookies
- Measuring instruments, bowls, pans needed for the recipe
- Boardmaker symbols with a word for each ingredient and action, such as mix, add, roll, bake, and so on
- Individual names of the students in a box (we use emptied wet wipes boxes)

Instructions

1. Write the recipe on chart paper, placing Boardmaker symbols beside the each ingredient or action.
2. Show each ingredient.
3. Explain each action.
4. Draw student name out of the box, and ask that student to do the instruction (e.g., "Jon, measure the sugar. Ann, pour the sugar in the bowl.").
5. Proceed through the recipe until it is complete.
6. While the cookies are baking, discuss different ways to use potatoes. Brainstorm other interesting items that can be used in making cookies.

Potato Chip Cookies

1 cup butter or margarine, softened

$\frac{1}{2}$ cup granulated sugar

1 teaspoon vanilla extract

2 cups all-purpose flour

1 cup potato chips, crushed

1. Preheat oven to 350 degrees.
2. In a large mixing bowl with an electric mixer at medium speed, cream butter, sugar, and vanilla. Add flour and potato chips.

3. Form dough into 1" balls and place on ungreased baking sheets. Press flat with the bottom of a glass dipped in sugar. Bake for 15 to 18 minutes or until golden.

Source: This recipe came from www.cooksrecipes.com

Snowflakes

This snowflake activity is fun and fanciful. Your students will experience success as they have fun creating and experimenting with the silvers, blues, and whites of winter. The pictures make a nice contribution to a wintry classroom atmosphere.

Materials

- Gray construction paper
- White school glue
- White and silver glitter
- Cardboard
- Blue food coloring
- Shallow containers such as disposable pie pans or polystyrene trays

Preparation

1. Cut strips of cardboard about 2" wide and in different lengths ($1\frac{1}{2}$"–3").

2. Mix food coloring into glue to make several different shades of blue (about a half cup of glue for each shade).

3. Pour each glue/food coloring mixture into a shallow container.

4. Make a model.

Instructions

1. Give each student a sheet of gray construction paper.

2. Show the model.

3. Show the students how to dip the long edge of the cardboard strips into the glue colors and then use the strips to stamp lines.

4. It is best to use the longer strips first, and then fill in with the shorter strips. Cross the lines at their center points to form a snowflake shape. Continue until they are similar to the spokes of a wheel.

5. Sprinkle with the white and/or silver glitter while still wet.

6. Lay flat to dry.

Vocabulary

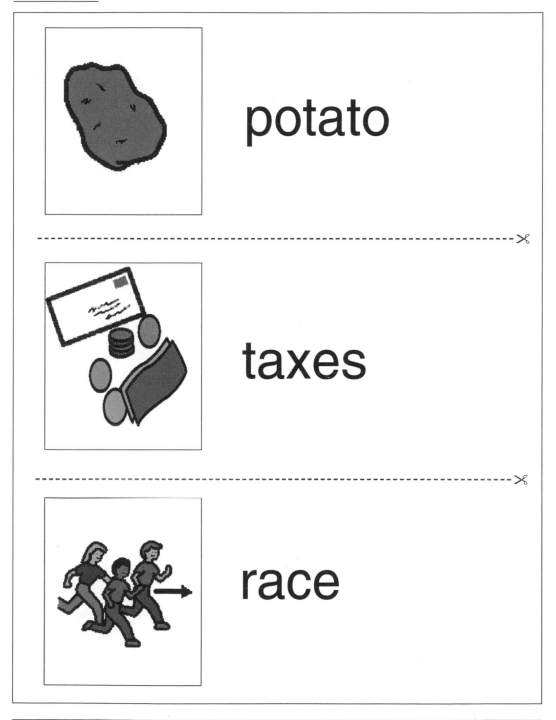

potato

taxes

race

winter

sled

worried

sadness

died

cold

frozen

grandfather

arctic

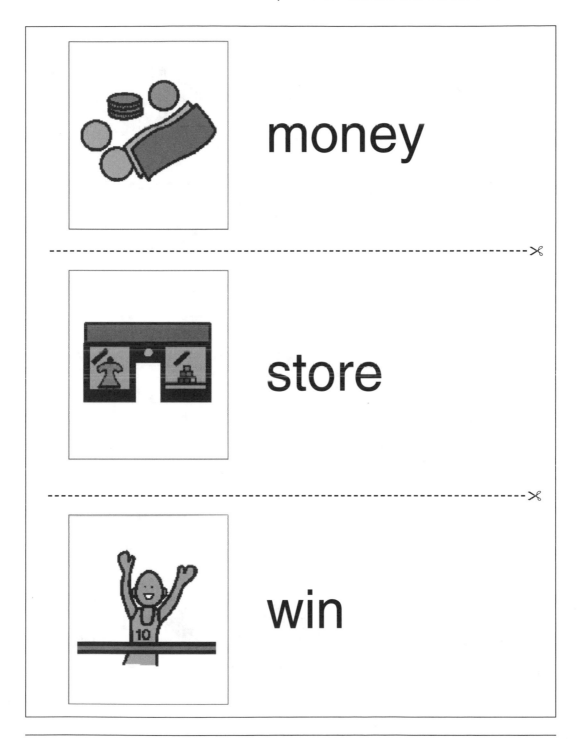

money

store

win

Communication Board

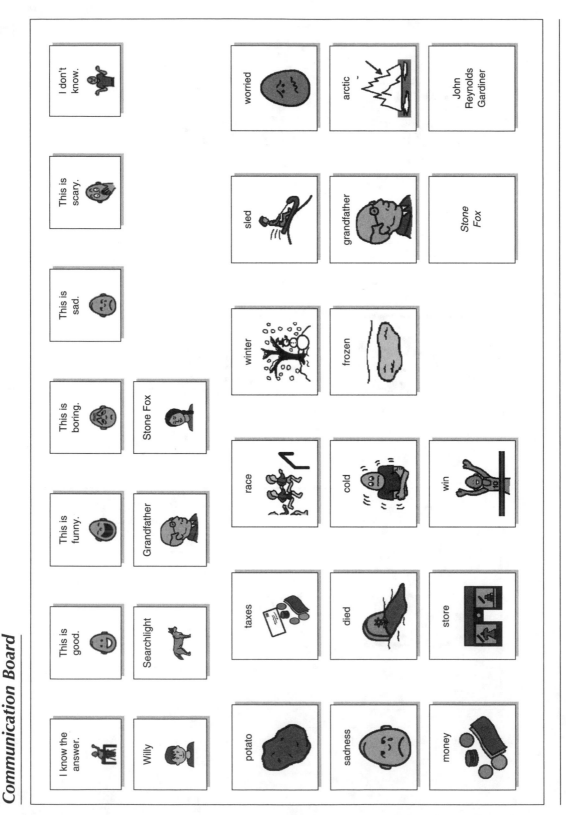

I know the answer.	This is good.	This is funny.	This is boring.	This is sad.	This is scary.	I don't know.
Willy	Searchlight	Grandfather	Stone Fox			

potato	taxes	race	winter	sled	worried
sadness	died	cold	frozen	grandfather	arctic
money	store	win		Stone Fox	John Reynolds Gardiner

THE WIZARD OF OZ LESSON PLAN

COMPONENTS

Summary of *The Wizard of Oz* by L. Frank Baum

Theme Plan

Making Roads

Poppies: Art Activity

Graphing Skittles: Math Activity

Vocabulary

Communication Board

Summary of The Wizard of Oz *by L. Frank Baum*

Dorothy is a young girl who lives with her Auntie Em and Uncle Henry and her dog Toto on a farm in Kansas. One day, the farmhouse, with Dorothy inside, is caught up in a cyclone and deposited in Munchkin Land. The house landed on the Wicked Witch of the East, killing her. The Good Witch of the North greets Dorothy and gives her a pair of ruby slippers. She tells Dorothy that she must go to the Emerald City and see the Wizard of Oz to ask for his help in returning her to Kansas.

Dorothy follows the yellow brick road to the Emerald City, and along the way she meets several interesting characters. She first meets the Scarecrow and frees him from the pole he is hanging on. The Scarecrow asks if he can join Dorothy on her journey so that he can ask the Wizard for a brain. They next meet the rusty Tin Woodman. Dorothy restores his movements by using an oilcan, and the Tin Woodman joins the group to ask the Wizard for a heart. Farther down the yellow brick road, they meet a Cowardly Lion, and Dorothy encourages him to come with them so that he can ask for courage.

The weary travelers finally reach the Emerald City to seek an audience with the Wizard. The Wizard agrees to help them achieve their goals, but he tells them that they must first kill the Wicked Witch of the West who rules over Winkie County. As the friends travel across Winkie County, the Wicked Witch sends animals and soldiers to attack them, but the friends manage to get past all of these obstacles. The Wicked Witch tricks Dorothy and gets one of her slippers, and in anger, Dorothy throws a bucket of water on the Witch, who melts.

Dorothy and her friends return to the Wizard again, and this time they discover that the Wizard is actually an old man who journeyed to Oz many years ago in a hot air balloon. The Wizard assures the Scarecrow, the Tin Man, and the Cowardly Lion that they are not lacking brains, a heart, or courage, but what they need is faith in themselves. Dorothy eventually meets Glinda, the Good Witch of the South, who tells her that she has always had the power to go home. The Ruby Slippers that she wears are magical and can take her anywhere she wishes to go just by clicking the heels together. The story ends as the Scarecrow returns to the Emerald City, the Tin Woodman goes to Winkie County, and the Cowardly Lion returns to the forest. Dorothy and Toto go home to Kansas for a happy reunion with her family.

Theme Plan

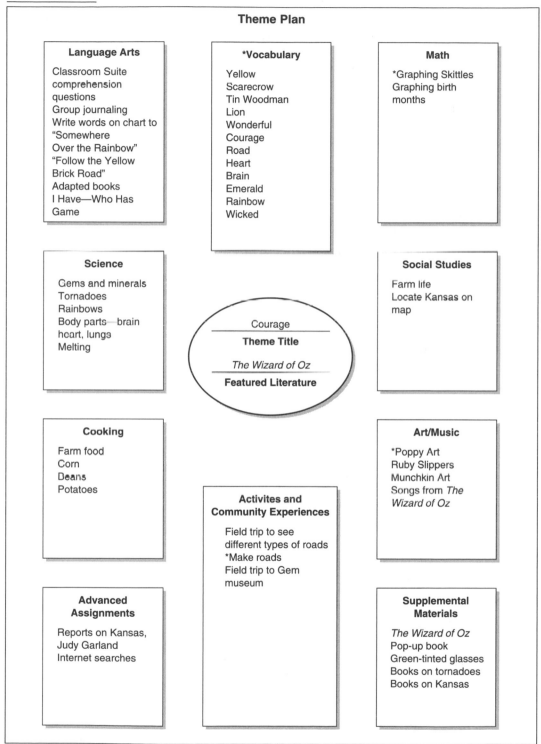

Theme Plan

Language Arts

Classroom Suite
comprehension
questions
Group journaling
Write words on chart to
"Somewhere
Over the Rainbow"
"Follow the Yellow
Brick Road"
Adapted books
I Have—Who Has
Game

*Vocabulary

Yellow
Scarecrow
Tin Woodman
Lion
Wonderful
Courage
Road
Heart
Brain
Emerald
Rainbow
Wicked

Math

*Graphing Skittles
Graphing birth
months

Science

Gems and minerals
Tornadoes
Rainbows
Body parts—brain
heart, lungs
Melting

Courage
Theme Title

The Wizard of Oz
Featured Literature

Social Studies

Farm life
Locate Kansas on
map

Cooking

Farm food
Corn
Beans
Potatoes

**Activites and
Community Experiences**

Field trip to see
different types of roads
*Make roads
Field trip to Gem
museum

Art/Music

*Poppy Art
Ruby Slippers
Munchkin Art
Songs from *The
Wizard of Oz*

**Advanced
Assignments**

Reports on Kansas,
Judy Garland
Internet searches

**Supplemental
Materials**

The Wizard of Oz
Pop-up book
Green-tinted glasses
Books on tornadoes
Books on Kansas

Making Roads

How fun it was to see the characters in *The Wizard of Oz* travel down the yellow brick road. In this lesson, students will learn about different types of roads, and then create a road of their choice. In the supplemental writing activity, the students write about where they would like their road to lead.

Materials

- Sheets of cardboard 12" × 18"
- Indoor/outdoor carpet that looks like grass cut into 12" × 12" squares
- Items that are used on the roads, such as:

  Dark gray sandpaper (looks like a paved road)
  River rocks
  Tile broken into pieces
  Linoleum that looks like bricks
  Dirt
  Sand

- Yellow paint
- Paintbrushes
- Rubber cement
- Heavy-duty scissors

Instructions

1. Hand out one sheet of cardboard and a piece of carpet to each student.

2. Ask students if they want a straight or curvy road, and cut carpet in half accordingly.

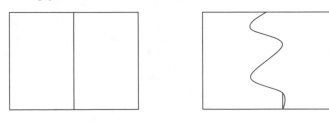

3. Ask the students what type of materials they want to use to make their road, such as gravel, dirt, brick, or pavement.

4. If the students want to make a "paved" road, let them glue the sandpaper down the middle of the cardboard. Pull apart the carpet so the edges of the carpet line up with the edges of the cardboard on each side.

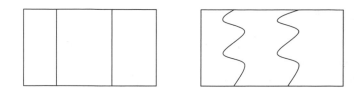

5. For all other materials, glue the separated carpet down first, and then add the materials to the middle of the board.

6. For the paved roads, have students paint yellow lines down the middle of the road.

Supplemental Writing Activity

Materials

- $8\frac{1}{2}" \times 11"$ paper with the following typed in large letters: I want my _____ road to take me to _____.
- Boardmaker symbols of different places students may want to go, such as the beach, swimming, the park, an amusement park, the library, home, and other places.

Instructions

1. Review the yellow brick road in *The Wizard of Oz* and how roads can lead to all different types of places.

2. Allow students to complete the first part of the sentence by writing (independently, hand over hand, by dictation, etc.) the type of road they chose.

3. Ask students where they would like their road to take them, and allow them to use Boardmaker symbols or independent writing to fill in the last blank.

4. After all students are finished, have each student show their road and read their completed sentence.

Poppies: Art Activity

The characters of *The Wizard of Oz* were delighted by the brilliant field of poppies. Students will be delighted with the beautiful artwork they produce as they follow the sequence of steps and use sponges to produce their own fields of poppies.

Materials

- Red, green, yellow, white, and black acrylic paint
- Art sponge
- White construction paper ($8\frac{1}{2}"\times 11"$)
- Paint rollers
- $\frac{1}{2}"$ and $\frac{3}{4}"$ circle sponges
- Shallow containers for paint
- Scissors

Preparation

1. Cut the sponge into the shape of poppy flowers.
2. Cut the construction paper sheets in half to make $4"\times 5\frac{1}{2}"$ sheets.
3. Mix a small amount of black paint into the red and green paint.
4. Put the green, red, and yellow paint in shallow containers.
5. Make a model for your students.

Instructions

1. Using the green paint and a roller, roll your background onto the paper.
2. Allow the green paint to dry slightly.
3. Stamp red poppies onto the background using the poppy-shaped sponges.
4. Allow the red paint to dry slightly.
5. Using the circle sponges, stamp the centers of the poppies with yellow paint.
6. Allow the yellow paint to dry slightly.
7. Using a stiff, small brush, highlight the yellow with tiny white strokes.
8. Allow pictures to dry completely before mounting.

Tips

Acrylic paint will stain clothing. Make sure that your students are wearing paint shirts or aprons.

These pictures look wonderful mounted on black paper.

Graphing Skittles: Math Activity

The students will enjoy the opportunity to determine which color of Skittles occurs most frequently while making rainbow graphs.

Materials

- White legal-size paper
- Crayons
- Yardstick
- Pencils
- Small bags of Skittles candy
- Chart paper

Preparation

1. Prepare blank graphs on the white legal paper by making five columns of 20 squares each.
2. Label the columns in the order of the rainbow: red, orange, yellow, green, and purple.
3. Prepare a paper chart for recording the large-group results by writing the color words red, orange, yellow, green, and purple across the bottom.

Instructions

1. Divide the students into groups of three or four. Give each group a blank graph, small bag of Skittles, and crayons.
2. Have each group count and graph their Skittles by coloring or placing the candies in the squares.
3. After the groups have completed graphing, call all small groups together into a large group.
4. Have a reporter from each small group report findings to the large group.
5. Use the chart paper to record the group findings using tally marks. Ask students to explain the results.

Vocabulary

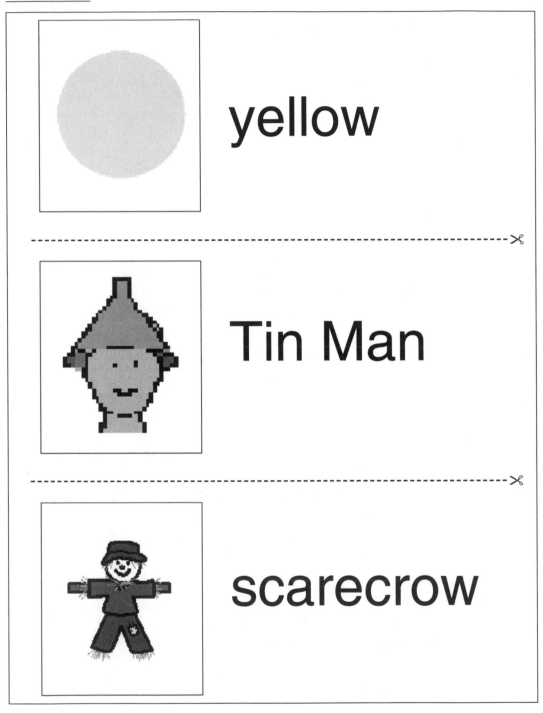

yellow

Tin Man

scarecrow

lion

courage

wonderful

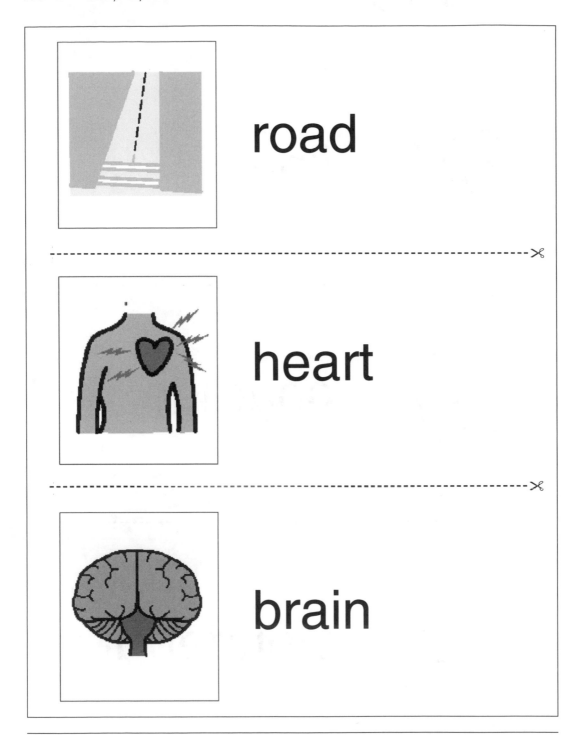

road

heart

brain

emerald

rainbow

wicked

Communication Board

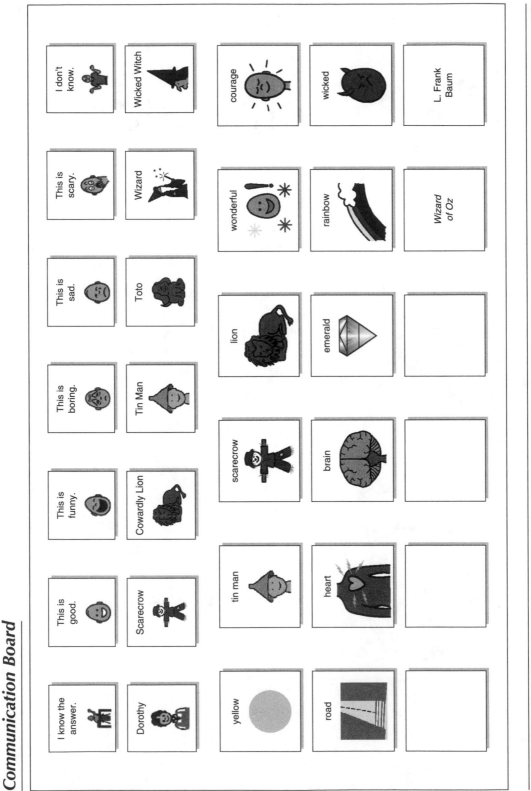

I know the answer.	This is good.	This is funny.	This is boring.	This is sad.	This is scary.	I don't know.
Dorothy	Scarecrow	Cowardly Lion	Tin Man	Toto	Wizard	Wicked Witch
yellow	tin man	scarecrow	lion	wonderful	courage	
road	heart	brain	emerald	rainbow	wicked	
				Wizard of Oz	L. Frank Baum	

Assistive Technology Planning Sheet

Student Name	Technology Needs

Suggested Individual Assistive Technology Tools

Objects

Photography

Picture Symbols (Boardmaker)

Talking Word Processor (Classroom Suite-IntelliTools)

Switch for Computer Mouse Access (Switch Click)

Adapted Keyboard (Intellikeys, Big Keys)

Adapted Reading Materials (PixWriter, Writing With Symbols)

Communication Devices

Adapted Books (BuildAbility, Classroom Suite)

Page Fluffers to Help Turn Book Pages

Activities Using IntelliTools Classroom Suite: Comprehension and Vocabulary

ACTIVITY PLANNING

Making Comprehension Activities Using *IntelliTools Classroom Suite*

This is a brief summary of how to create a reading comprehension activity. More detailed instructions are available in the Classroom Suite manual.

1. Open a NEW writing program. (In Classroom Suite 4 you find a writing program by first choosing the CREATIVITY TOOLS and then selecting WRITING TOOLS.)

2. Type the fill-in-the-blank questions with an answer field at the end of each question.

3. Lock the text.

4. Create a toolbar with the number of buttons equal to the number of questions.

5. Add a BUTTON NAME and PICTURE that represents the answer to one of the questions. The action for the button is INSERT PICTURE OR NAME.

6. Create a toolbar with buttons for tools that include READ, DELETE WORD, and PRINT. The actions for these buttons represent the desired task.

7. Save.

Making Vocabulary Activities Using *IntelliTools Classroom Suite*

This is a brief summary of how to create a vocabulary activity. More detailed instructions are available in the Classroom Suite manual.

1. Open a NEW writing program. (In Classroom Suite 4 you find a writing program by first choosing the CREATIVITY TOOLS tab and then selecting WRITING TOOLS.)

2. Create a toolbar with buttons for each of the new vocabulary words.

3. Add a picture to each button. The action will be TYPE TEXT and include the definition of the vocabulary word.

4. In the OPTIONS menu, click on SPEAK SENTENCES.

5. As the student clicks on a button representing a vocabulary word, the definition will appear on the screen and the text will be read to the student.

Web Resources for Literacy Support

Resources to support and enrich the classroom experience, with a focus on helping teachers build experiences in language and ensure that our instruction is accessible to all students.

www.aacintervention.com. Lots of great reading, writing, and augmentative communication strategies.

www.adaptedlearning.com. A site to find, share, and use materials created by therapists, teachers, and families. This site is hosted by Mayer-Johnson.

www.closingthegap.com. Excellent resource on the latest assistive technology trends. This site has a free online discussion forum.

www.intellitools.com. Click on the Activity Exchange for hundreds of activities created by teachers and therapists. You will need to have Classroom Suite to use these activities.

www.fullmeasure.co.uk/powertalk. PowerTalk provides automatic speech for PowerPoint presentations.

www.lindaburkhart.com. Valuable site with useful information for AAC users and tips on teaching switch use.

www.literactive.com. Reading materials for Pre–K to first-grade students, including leveled, guided readers and phonics activities.

www.nationalgeographic.com/ngyoungexplorer. Online support for the classroom magazine *National Geographic Young Explorer!*

www.priorywoods.middlesbrough.sch.uk. Click on the resources link then click on Interactive Talking Story Books. Here you will find a good Big Book Template created in MS PowerPoint.

www.starfall.com. Online alphabet lessons and simple stories. Good for beginning mouse users.

www.storylineonline.net. The Members of the Screen Actors Guild read their favorite books.

www.storyplace.org. Web site for the Charlotte, North Carolina, library system. The stories are read for the students, and the site offers worksheets. Spanish stories are also available.

http://streaming.discoveryeducation.com. This is a digital video-on-demand and online teaching service.

Glossary

Age-appropriate Activities and materials that are appropriate for and commonly enjoyed by persons of a certain age.

Assistive or adaptive technology "Products, devices or equipment, whether acquired commercially, modified or customized, that are used to maintain, increase, or improve the functional capabilities of individuals with disabilities" (Assistive Technology Act, 2004, Section 3).

Alternative or augmentative communication (AAC) Forms of communication (not including oral speech) that help an individual express needs, ideas, feelings, and wants. It is usually used by individuals with severe speech or language disabilities. The alternative or augmentative system may be sign language, symbols, objects, communication devices or boards, pictures, or gestures.

Brainstorming Providing individuals opportunities to discuss new ideas by unrestricted, spontaneous participation in discussion.

Embedded Individual instruction taught within the context of group instruction.

Emergent level Skill level preceding the conventional literacy level.

Expressive language Language used to convey wants, needs, and ideas. Expressive language can be oral, sign language, picture symbols, voice-output devices, gestures, and so on.

Functional skills Performing basic skills related to self-care or work tasks.

Graphic organizer A drawing used to arrange elements in order to teach a theme. It is also referred to as a *planning web*.

Guided reading A strategy in which the teacher is the facilitator, pointing out key elements in the story and building on the students' background knowledge. This instruction may occur for the purpose of teaching word identification skills and increasing oral reading fluency, as well as developing comprehension skills.

High-tech assistive technology devices Assistive technology devices that perform several functions. For example, a high-tech device might be a computer that contains communication software with extensive vocabulary, Internet access, and environmental controls.

Individual education plan (IEP) A plan written by a student and the student's team, including teachers and parents, to design appropriate individual goals for the coming school year.

Inclusion A student with disabilities taking part in activities with his or her nondisabled peers.

Interdisciplinary services Accessing ideas and expertise from a variety of staff members available in a school setting. This group includes counselors, speech pathologists, occupational therapists, physical therapists, music teachers, and art teachers, among others.

Journaling Writing about daily activities and events.

Literacy skills Skills needed to read, write, and use language

Listening comprehension level Complexity of language that is easily understood by a listener.

Low-tech assistive technology communication devices Simple assistive devices that are easy to design or program and contain a limited vocabulary set.

Multilevel Instruction designed such that the needs of all children are considered.

Multimedia A variety of teaching tools, such as the Internet, videos, data projectors, overhead projectors, and so on. These tools can also be used by students to demonstrate their knowledge of a topic.

Multimethod Utilizing different ways of teaching, such as games, hands-on materials, visual charts, sign language, and so on.

Multisensory Instruction or learning activities that include the use of two or more sensory modalities (such as auditory, visual, and kinesthetic) at the same time.

No Child Left Behind (NCLB) Implemented during the 2002–2003 school year, this act requires schools to have 100% proficiency among students in math, reading, and language arts by 2014. Students must also meet graduation and attendance standards.

Nonverbal The minimal use of intelligible verbal language.

Page fluffers Handmade adaptations attached to the edge of a page to make it easier to turn, assisting with fine motor control. Examples are pieces of Styrofoam, paper clips, or card stock attached to the edge of the page.

Peer tutors Regular education students who spend a class period a day in the special education classroom.

Planning web Organizational tool used to plan thematic units. It is also referred to as a *graphic organizer*.

Presentations Reports by students related to topics being studied.

Qwerty keyboard Traditional typewriter keyboard. *Qwerty* refers to the letters on the top row of the keyboard starting at the left.

Receptive language Language understood by the listener.

Retelling Restating a story in a student's own words.

Sharing the pen Students are given an opportunity to interact and contribute during a group writing lessons by writing letters or words or by attaching symbols, photographs, or objects.

Standard course of study (SCS) Required curriculum designed by individual states' boards of education.

Thematic instruction Integrated learning of reading, writing, listening, and speaking in all subject areas centered on a single unit of instruction.

Thinking out loud A teaching model on how to write. The teacher orally states the thinking process while writing it down. This allows the child to hear the adult thought process as the adult is converting the thoughts into print.

Time delay technique During a trial, give a natural cue and prompt for the answer. Gradually increase delay between the cue and the prompt, giving reinforcement for correct answers.

Transitional text Reading *with* beginning readers to support simple word attack strategies.

Whole language "Language across the curriculum," meaning that reading and writing are incorporated in all subject areas, such as history and science. Children are taught the "how to" of the reading process rather than individual segments presented in isolated ways.

Word wall Frequently occurring words in reading or the school environment. These words are displayed on a bulletin board in the classroom.

References

LIST OF UNIVERSAL RESOURCE LOCATORS

Chapter 4: http://thewizardofoz.warnerbros.com/cmp/cpic20.htm
Chapter 6: http://crafts.kaboose.com/ice-cream-in-a-bag.html
Chapter 8: http://www.ncpublicschools.org/curriculum/ncecs

PUBLISHED MATERIALS

Allinder, R. (2000). Effects of teacher self-monitoring on implementation of curriculum-based measurement and mathematics computation achievement of students with disabilities. *Remedial & Special Education, 21*(4), 219–227.

Alton, S. (1998). Differentiation not discrimination: Delivering the curriculum for children with Down's syndrome in mainstream schools. *Support for Learning, 13*(4), 167–173.

Assistive Technology Act of 2004, Public Law 108–364, 108th Cong. (2004). Retrieved June 13, 2008, from http://www.resna.org/taproject/library/laws/p1108–364.pdf

Basil, C., & Reyes, S. (2003). Acquisition of literacy skills by children with severe disabilities [Electronic version]. *Child Language Teaching and Therapy, 19*(1), 27–48.

Blatt, B., & Keplan, F. (1966). *Christmas in purgatory: A photographic essay on mental retardation.* Boston: Allyn & Bacon.

Browder, D., & Cooper-Duffy, K. (2003). Evidence-based practices for students with severe disabilities and the requirement for accountability in "No Child Left Behind." *Journal of Special Education, 37*(3), 157–164.

Browder, D., Wakeman, S., Spooner, F., Ahlgrim-Delzell, L., & Algozzine, B. (2006). Research on reading instruction for individuals with significant cognitive disabilities. *Exceptional Children, 72*(4), 392–408.

Burkart, G., & Sheppard, K. (n.d.). A descriptive study of content-ESL practices, volume III: Training packet material. (Contract no. T291004001, Task 19.3). Washington, DC: U.S. Department of Education's Office of Bilingual Education and Minority Languages Affairs. (ERIC Clearinghouse on Urban Education). Retrieved March 23, 2008, from http://www.ncela.gwu.edu/pubs/cal/contentesl/index.htm

Collins, B., & Griffen, A. K. (1996). Teaching students with moderate disabilities to make safe responses to product warning labels. *Education & Treatment of Children, 19*(1), 30–46.

Cromwell, S. (1997). Whole language and phonics: Can they work together? *Education World.* Retrieved November 13, 2008, from http://education-world.com/a_curr/curr029.shtml

Cunningham, P., & Allington, R. (2007). *Classrooms that work: They can all read and write.* Boston: Pearson Education.

Dattmer, P., Dyck, N., &Thurston, L. (1999). *Consultation, collaboration, and teamwork.* Boston: Allyn & Bacon.

Downing, J. (2005). *Teaching literacy to students with significant disabilities: Strategies for the k–12 inclusive classroom.* Thousand Oaks, CA: Corwin.

Erickson, K. A., & Hanser, G. A. (2004). *Writing with alternative pencils* [CD-ROM]. Chapel Hill: The Center for Literacy & Disability Studies, University of North Carolina.

Faykus, S., & McCurdy, B. (1998). Evaluating the sensitivity of the maze as an index of reading proficiency for students who are severely deficient in reading. *Education & Treatment of Children, 21*(1), 1–21.

Gardiner, J. R. (1983). *Stone Fox.* New York: Harper Collins.

Hanser, G. A. (2006). *Predictable chart writing.* Handout. Chapel Hill: The Center for Literacy and Disability Studies, University of North Carolina.

Hyperstudio by Roger Wagner®, a registered trademark of Roger Wagner Publishing, Inc.

IntelliTools®, a registered trademark of IntelliTools, Inc.

Kostelnik, M. (Ed.). (1996). *Themes teachers use.* Glenview, IL: GoodYear Books.

IntelliTools®, a registered trademark of IntelliTools, Inc.

Longacre, D. J. (1976). *More-with-less cookbook.* Scottdale, PA: Herald Press.

Mesibov, G. (n.d.). *Learning styles of students with autism.* Retrieved July 7, 2005, from http://www.teacch.com/learningstyles.mtml

Morocco, C., Hindin, A., Mata-Aguilar, D., & Clark-Chiarelli, N. (2001). Building a deep understanding of literature with middle-grade students with learning disabilities [Electronic version]. *Learning Disability Quarterly, 24*(4), 47–58.

Northwest Regional Educational Laboratory. (n.d.). Focus on effectiveness: Research-based instruction. *Thematic instruction.* Retrieved June 13, 2008, from http://www.netc.org/focus/strategies/them.php

On Purpose Associates. (1998–2001). Thematic instruction. *Funderstanding.* Retrieved January 14, 2006, from http://www.funderstanding.com/thematic_instruction.cfm

Pitcher, S., & Mackey, B. (2004). *Collaborating for real literacy: Librarian, teacher, and principal.* Worthington, OH: Linworth.

PowerPoint®, a registered trademark of Microsoft Corporation.

Routman, R. (1988). *Transitions from literature to literacy.* Melbourne, Australia: Rigby.

Scott, V., & Weishaar, M. (2003). Curriculum-based measurement for reading progress. *Intervention in School & Clinic, 38*(3), 153–160.

Skittles®, a registered trademark of Mars, Incorporated.

Sulzby, E., & Barnhart, J. (1992). The development of academic competence: All our children emerge as writers and readers. In J. W. Irwin & M. A. Doyle (Eds.), *Reading and writing connections: Learning from research* (pp. 120–144). Newark, DE: International Reading Association.

Stecker, P., & Fuchs, L. (2000). Effecting superior achievement using curriculum-based measurement: The importance of individual progress monitoring. *Learning Disabilities Research & Practices, 15*(3), 128–134. Retrieved February 14, 2005, from http://online2.wcu.edu8900/SCRIPT/SPED631_15_042/scripts/serve_home

Sulkes, S. (2006). Mental retardation/intellectual disability. In *Merck manuals online medical library.* Retrieved June 12, 2008, from http://www.merck.com/mmhe/sec23/ch285/ch285a.html

The Picture Communication Symbols © 1981–2008 by Mayer-Johnson LLC, P.O. Box 1579, Solana Beach, CA 92075, USA, Phone: 858-550-0084, Fax: 858-550-0449, Email: mayerj@mayer-johnson.com, Web site: http://www.mayer-johnson.com

Wagner, D. K., Musselwhite, C. R., & Odom, J. (2005). Facilitating communication. In *Out & about: AAC in the community* [CD-ROM]. Litchfield Park, AZ: AAC Intervention. (Available from www.aacintervention.com)

Walt Disney Feature Animation (Producer), Balise, A., & Walker, R. (Directors). (2003). *Brother bear* [Motion picture]. United States: Walt Disney Feature Animation.

Westling, D., & Fox, L. (2004). *Teaching students with severe disabilities* (3rd ed). Upper Saddle River, NJ: Pearson Prentice Hall.

Winterling, V. (1990). The effects of constant time delay, practice in writing or spelling, and reinforcement on sight word recognition in a small group. *Journal of Special Education, 24*(1), 101–117.

Yolen, J. (1987). *Owl Moon.* New York: Penguin Group, USA.

Index

AbleNet, Inc., 51 (table)
Access, 4, 14, 16, 23, 40, 48, 58, 105
Accessibility features, 50, 51–53 (table), 56
Activities
    art, 114–115, 151–152, 177–178
    bingo, 133
    calendar skills, 112–113
    chapter read aloud, 110
    different types of races, 164
    family tree, 150–151
    field trip, 29–30, 153–155
    graphing, 92, 111–112, 179
    invitation writing, 115–116
    journaling, 109–110
    jungle mural, 123
    list making, 113
    make an island, 137–138
    making roads, 176–177
    model journaling, 108–109
    mountain views, 151–152
    nonstandard measurement and
        estimation, 124–125
    planning, 29–30
    poppies, 177–178
    potato chip cookies, 165–166
    potato print pictures, 114–115
    predictable chart writing, 114
    quilt day, 152–153
    sand casting, 141–142
    snowflakes, 166
    social studies, 118, 150–151
    stone soup, 153–155
    structuring, 36–37
    tornado in a bottle, 125–126
    using IntelliTools Classroom Suite, 186
    vocabulary lesson, 110–111, 186
    weather, 126–127
    word game, 110
    writing, 117, 177

Adapted books, 185
Adaptive technology. *See* Assistive or
    adaptive technology
Advanced assignments, 77–79
Age-appropriate materials, 2–3
Age-appropriate literature, 5
    choosing, 25–26
    planning for use of, 19–21
    theme teaching and, 7–8, 19
Ahlgrim-Delzell, L., 4
Aladdin, 76 (photo)
Algozzine, B., 4
Allinder, R., 6
Allington, R., 69
Alphabet flip charts, 49
Alternative and augmentative
    communication (AAC), 43, 48
Alternative Pencils, 49
Alton, S., 13
AMDI, Inc., 51 (table)
Angelman's syndrome, 12
Apple Corporation, 50
Art lessons, 114–115, 151–152, 177–178
Assessment
    checklist, 98
    data collection for, 88, 89–91 (table)
    games for, 94–98
    graphing exercises for, 92
    individualized education plans (IEP)
        and, 87–88, 89–91 (table)
    individual journaling for, 85–86
    planning for, 29
    retelling as, 94
    See also Instructional delivery
Assignments, advanced, 77–79
Assistive or adaptive technology, 21, 33
    accessibility features, 50,
        51–53 (table), 56
    assessment and, 94

communication, 53–56
computers as, 48–49
defined, 47
digital books, 50
planning, 33
planning sheet, 185
preparing, 43–45
writing aids, 48–49
Assistive Technology, Inc., 51 (table)
Attainment Co., Inc., 50, 51 (table)
Auditory processing difficulties, 22 (table)
Augmentative and alternative
communication (AAC), 43, 48
Autism, 12, 21, 37

Barnhart, J., 19
Basil, C., 6
Behavior, 2, 30
Big Keys, 185
Bingo, 133
Black Hawks, 44
Black Stallion, The, 20, 62, 77
bingo, 133
Classroom Suite web page, 134
communication board, 132
group teaching and, 126–127
jungle mural activity, 123
lesson plan, 121–134
nonstandard measurement and
estimation activity, 124–125
summary, 121
theme plan, 122
tornado in a bottle activity, 125–126
vocabulary, 128–131
Boardmaker, 185
Boards
communication, 132, 147,
161, 172, 184
white, 45, 115
Books
adapted, 185
chapter read aloud, 110
digital, 50
language, 53–56
retelling, 60–66
selection of, 25–26
See also Literature
Boxes, name, 46
Braille alphabet flip charts, 49
Braille Intellikeys Overlay, 49
Brainstorming, 26, 62
Breaks, scheduling, 37–39
Browder, D., 4, 6

Brown Bear, Brown Bear, What Do You
See?, 20
BuildAbility, 45, 50, 185
Building a theme. See Thematic units
Burrill, M., 75 (photo)

Calendar skills, 105, 112–113, 115
Cerebral palsy, 12
Challenges, 3, 12–13, 16, 20, 22 (table)
Chambers, A., 21
Chapter read aloud, 110
Characteristics, 3, 12–13,
Charts
flip, 49
instruction, 37
tablets, large, 45, 70
writing, predictable, 72–74, 114
Child Language Teaching and Therapy, 5
Christmas in Purgatory, 1
Cinderella, 75 (photo), 100
Clark-Chiarelli, N., 7
Classroom environment, 36
checklist, 46
enhancement, 39–41
hands-on learning materials and, 41–43
literature brought life in, 74,
75–76 (photo)
materials, 45–46
Classroom Suite, 44, 45, 48, 50, 94
in lesson plans, 134, 185, 186
Cleaning skills, 105
Cleaver, Bill, 18
Cleaver, V., 18
Collection of data, 88, 89–91 (table)
Collins, B., 6
Color-Coded Eye-Gaze Frames, 49
Communicate, 28, 45, 48, 53, 55, 102
Communication
assistive or adaptive
technology, 53–56
augmentative and alternative, 43, 48
boards, 132, 147, 161, 172, 184
devices, 21
facilitators, 43–44
notebooks, 44, 54–55 (photo), 55, 60,
63 (photo), 67, 86, 110, 116
symbols, 29, 37, 40, 44, 59, 67, 77, 94,
102, 104–105,111
objects, 37, 48, 77
nonverbal, 12, 43, 46, 48, 62, 77, 83, 94,
partners, 44
with parents, 30–33, 139–140, 152–153
verbal, 21, 62, 77,

Community experiences, 29–30, 72
Comprehension, 7–8, 16, 21, 26, 44–45, 58,
  60, 66, 69, 71, 79, 86, 92, 94, 97
Computers, 48–49, 56
  accessibility features, 50, 51–53 (table)
  digital books and, 50
  keyboards, 49, 55, 56, 62, 63 (photo), 185
  mouse access, 185
  talking word processor, 185Conceptual
    glue, 18, 70, 108
Connect to prior learning, 109–112,
  114–115, 117
Consolidation and retention of learning
  difficulties, 22 (table)
Consultation, Collaboration and
  Teamwork, 18
Cookies, potato chip, 165–166
Cooking skills, 104, 165–166
Cooper-Duffy, K., 6
Course of study, standard, 87, 120
Cri Du Chat syndrome, 12
Cromwell, S., 3
Cunningham, P., 69, 72
Curriculum-based
  measurements (CBM), 6

Dandy Walker syndrome, 12
Data
  collection, 88, 89–91 (table)
  sheets, 46, 61, 87–88,
    89–91 (table), 93 (table)
Development, program, 2–3
Different types of races, 164
Digital books, 50Distractibility, 22 (table)
Don Johnston, Inc., 51 (table)
Downing, June, 21
Down syndrome, 12, 13
DVDs, 26, 56
Dynavox, 44, 48, 51 (table), 62

Easels, three-legged, 45
Education & Treatment of Children, 5
ELMO Company LTD., 50, 51 (table)
Embedded goals, 29, 87
Emergent level, 19, 65, 109
Enabling Devices, 52 (table)
Enrichment, 17, 28, 41, 100, 102
Entries, retelling, 66
Environment, classroom, 36
  enhancement, 39–41
  hands-on learning materials and, 41–43
  literature brought to life in, 74,
    75–76 (photo)

Estimation and nonstandard
  measurement, 124–125
Events, scheduling, 30
Eye-gaze systems, 48, 49
Families, 8–9, 25, 30–31,
  46, 77, 81–83

Family tree, 150–151
Faykus, S., 7
Field trips, 29–30, 153–155
Fine motor skills, 12, 22 (table), 36, 123
Flip charts, 49
Fox, L., 13
Fuchs, L., 6
Functional skills, 104–105

Games, 94–98, 110
General education
  checklist, 103
  defined, 99
  special education teachers working with
    teachers in, 100–102
Generalization, 13, 16, 68, 82
Goals
  embedded, 29, 87
  individual, 29, 61
Government mandates, 2
Graphic organizers, 26–28, 33
Graphing, 92, 111–112, 179
Griffen, A. K., 6
Group teaching, 126–127
Guided reading, 69–71, 116

Hands-on learning, 41–43
Hanser, G., 49, 72
Head pointers, computer, 49
Highlighting, 45
  tape, 45–46
High-tech assistive technology, 21
Hindin, A., 7
Home involvement
  checklist for, 84
  communication for, 30–33, 139–140,
    152–153
  helping with presentations and, 83
  parent letter, 31, 83, 108, 139
  parent lobbying and, 2
  sharing the retelling and, 82
  sharing the vocabulary and, 82–83
Hyperstudio, 50
Inclusion, 99–102
Independence, 8, 9, 48
Independent, 1, 62, 65–66, 79

Individualized education plans (IEP), 11, 87
 data collection and, 88, 89–91 (table)
 goals data sheets, 92, 93 (table)
Individual journaling, 85–86, 109–110
Instructional delivery
 advanced assignments, 77–79
 building language, 71–72
 checklist, 80
 community experiences in, 29–30, 72
 functional skills, 104–105
 games in, 94–98
 guided reading, 69–71
 predictable chart writing, 72–74
 retelling in, 60–66, 82, 94
 sharing literature chapter-by-chapter, 60
 sharing the pen in, 65
 student presentations, 77, 83, 138–139
 theme introduction, 57–59
 vocabulary instruction, 67–69, 82–83
 vocabulary introduction, 59
 word walls for, 65–66
 See also Assessment; Thematic units
Intellectual disabilities, 5
Intellikeys, 185
IntelliTools, 48, 50, 52 (table),
  56 (photo), 185, 186
 assessment and, 94
 instructional delivery and, 82
 setting the stage and, 44
Interdisciplinary, 14
Internet, the, 50, 56
Introductions
 theme, 57–59
 vocabulary, 59
Invitation writing, 115–116
IQ (intelligence quotient) categories, 5
Island of the Blue Dolphins
 communication board, 147
 instructional delivery, 77, 83, 92
 lesson plan, 135–147
 make an island activity, 137–138
 parent letter, 139–140
 planning, 20
 sand casting activity, 141–142
 setting the stage, 41
 student presentations, 138–139
 summary, 135
 theme plan, 136
 vocabulary, 143–146

Journaling
 individual, 85–86, 109–110
 model, 108–109

Journal of Special Education, 5
Jungle Book, The, 58, 78 (photo)
Jungle mural, 123

Ken-a-Vision, Inc., 50, 52 (table)
Keyboards, computer, 49, 56, 185
 QWERTY, 55, 62, 63 (photo)
Key guards, computer, 49
Key Technologies, 52 (table)
Kurzweil Educational Systems, 48

Language
 books, 53–56
 building, 71–72
 expressive, 10, 48, 71
 of literature, 20–21
 receptive, 10, 71
 whole, 3, 57
 See also Vocabulary
Large chart tablets, 45, 70
Learning
 hands-on, 41–43
 styles and characteristics, 12–13, 22
  (table)
Learning Disabilities
 Research & Practice, 5
Learning Disability Quarterly, 5
Lesson plans
 Black Stallion, The 121–134
 Island of the Blue Dolphins, 135–147
 Stone Fox, 162–172
 weekly thematic, 108–118
 Where the Lilies Bloom, 148–161
 Wizard of Oz, The 173–184
 See also Planning, literacy program
Librarians, school, 14–15
Listening comprehension
 level, 26, 44, 60, 66, 71
List making, 113
Literacy skills
 learning challenges/implications
  and, 22 (table)
 program overview, premise,
  and goal, 9
 program principles, 9–10
 research on techniques for
  improving, 6–7
 theme teaching, 7–8
 See also Programs, literacy
Literature
 age-appropriate, 5, 7–8, 19–21
 brought to life, 74, 75–76 (photo)
 choosing, 25–26

language of, 20–21
retelling, 60–66
shared chapter-by-chapter, 60
See also Books
Little House on the Prairie, 42
Little Red Riding Hood, 20
Lobbying, parent, 2
Low-tech assistive technology, 21
for communication, 53–56

Magnetic word banks, 48
Making roads activity, 176–177
Mandates, government, 2
Markers, 45
Mata-Aguilar, D., 7
Materials, classroom, 45–46
Math activities, 92, 111–112, 179
Mayer-Johnson, LLC, 52 (table)
McCurdy, B., 7
Measurement and estimation,
    nonstandard, 124–125
Medications, 30
Merck Manual Online Medical Library, 5
Mesibov, G., 13
Microsoft, 50
Mimio, 52 (table)
Model, 37, 49, 59, 61, 66, 73, 77
Model journaling, 108–109
Money skills, 105
Morocco, C., 7
Mountain views, 151–152
Multilevel approach, 10, 16,
    28, 67, 70, 77, 79
Multimedia, 10, 164
Multimethod approach, 10
Multisensory learning, 10, 50
Musselwhite, C. R., 43
My Own Bookshelf, 50
My Side of the Mountain, 100, 101

Name(s)
    boxes, 46
    writing, 105
National Geographic Explorer!, 69
Neverending Story, The, 40, 76 (photo)
No Child Left Behind, 2
Nonstandard measurement and
    estimation, 124–125
Nonverbal students, 12, 21, 43, 46, 48, 62,
    77, 83, 94, 153
Notebooks, communication, 44,
    54–55 (photo), 55, 60, 63 (photo),
    67, 86, 110, 116

Objects as assistive technology tools, 185
Occupational therapists, 16, 45
Odom, J., 43
Organizational difficulties, 22 (table)
Out and About: AAC in the
    Community, 43
Outsiders, The, 26
Owl Moon, 108

Packing for community experiences, 30
Page Fluffers, 185
Parents
    checklist for home involvement by, 84
    communication with, 30–33, 139–140,
        152–153
    helping with presentations, 83
    lobbying, 2
    sharing the retelling with, 82
    sharing the vocabulary with, 82–83
Peer tutors, 61, 102, 103 (photo)
Pen, sharing the, 65
Pencil grips, 48
Personal hygiene skills, 105
Photography, 185
Physical education teachers, 16
Physical therapists, 16
Piaget, J., 19
Picture symbols, 185
PixWriter, 185
Planning
    age-appropriate literature and, 19–21
    aids, 33
    assessments and, 29
    assistive or adaptive technology, 33, 185
    basic principles, 12
    brainstorming in, 26
    community experiences and, 29–30
    finalizing, 29–30
    graphic organizers in, 26–28
    sheets, 33
    standard course of study, 120
    team approach to, 14–18
    technology and, 21, 43–45
    thematic approach to, 18–19, 24–25, 119
    time for, 17–18
    understanding the students when, 12–13
    web, 26–28
    See also Lesson plans
Poppies, 177–178
Potato chip cookies, 165–166
Potato print pictures, 114–115
PowerPoint, 50, 82
Prader Willi syndrome, 12

Predictable chart writing, 72–74, 114
Prentke Romich, 52 (table)
Presentations, 77, 78 (photo), 138–139
  parents helping with, 83
Print, 59, 66, 82
Probe, 73, 114
Programs, literacy
  age-appropriate literature and, 19–21
  development, 2–3
  overview, premise, and goal, 9
  planning principles, 12
  principles, 9–10
  team approach to, 14–18
  technology and, 21
  thematic approach to, 18–19
  understanding the students when
    planning, 12–13
  See also Literacy skills
Prompt, 61–62, 66–67, 111

Quilt day, 152–153
QWERTY keyboards, 55, 62, 63 (photo)

Races, different types of, 164
Read aloud, chapter, 110
Reading
  guided, 69–71, 116
  materials, adapted, 185
  self-selected, 108–110
Recorded-speech devices, 48
Remedial & Special Education, 5
Research in instruction of special needs
  students, 4–8
Retelling, 60–66
  as assessment, 94
  sharing the, 82
Retention and consolidation of learning
  difficulties, 22 (table)
Reyes, S., 6
Rhett syndrome, 12
RJ Cooper Company, 53 (table)
Routman, R., 20

Sand casting, 141–142
Sarason, S., 1
Schedules
  break, 37–39
  event, 30
  individual student, 37
Secret Garden, The, 58
Selection
  book, 25–26
  vocabulary, 28–29

Self-selected reading, 108–110
Sequencing problems, 22 (table)
Sharing
  literature chapter-by-chapter, 60
  the pen, 65
  the retelling, 82
  the vocabulary, 82–83
Significant Disabilities, 3–4, 6, 9–12, 14, 19,
  21–22 (table), 23, 25–26, 28, 30, 35, 37,
  45, 47, 49, 70–71, 77, 79
Skills
  functional, 104–105
  list making, 113
  synthesis, 22 (table)
  writing, 112–113, 115, 177
  See also Activities
Slater Software, 53 (table)
Snowflakes, 166
Social studies lessons, 118, 150–151
Sound, 55, 62, 66–67, 77, 82
Speech/language delays, 22 (table)
Speech/language pathologists, 16, 44
Special needs, 1–2, 9–13, 28–29, 47, 56, 77
Spooner, F., 4
Staff, 14, 29–30, 36, 46, 59–62, 66–68, 77,
  82–88, 113, 116, 124, 138–139
Standard course of study (SCS), 87, 120
Standards, 9-12, 23-29
Stecker, P., 6
Stimuli, 13, 22 (table)
Stone Fox, 20, 31–33, 56 (photo), 101
  assessment, 92
  communication board, 172
  different types of races activity, 164
  instructional delivery, 63–64,
    68, 78 (photo)
  lesson plan, 108, 118, 162–172
  potato chip cookies activity, 165–166
  snowflakes activity, 166
  summary, 162
  theme plan, 163
  vocabulary, 167–171
Stone Soup, 153–155
Structure
  activities, 36–37
  classroom environment, 36, 39–41
  providing, 35–36
Students
  challenges/implications and
    solutions for, 22 (table)
  functional skills, 104–105
  government mandates on, 2
  homework, 81

inclusion of, 99–102
increased awareness of, 1–2
individual goals, 59, 61
individualized education plans (IEP)
    for, 11, 87–88, 89–91 (table),
    92, 93 (table)
individual journaling by, 85–86, 109–110
individual schedules, 37
IQ levels of, 5
learning styles and characteristics
    of, 12, 22 (table)
nonverbal, 12, 21, 43, 46, 48, 62, 77, 83,
    94, 153
parent lobbying on behalf of, 2
peer tutors, 61, 102, 103 (photo)
presentations by, 77, 78 (photo),
    83, 138–139
program development for, 2–3
research on instruction of, 4–8
sharing the vocabulary, 82–83
understanding, 12–13
Study, standard course of, 87, 120
Support, 5, 9, 12–16, 36, 62, 79–81
Sulzby, E., 19
Swiss Family Robinson, The, 74
Switch Click, 185
Switches, computer, 49, 185

Tablets, large chart, 45
Tape, highlighting, 45–46
Tash, Inc., 53 (table)
Team approach to literacy programs,
    14–18
Technology, assistive or adaptive, 21, 33
    accessibility features,
        50, 51–53 (table), 56
    assessment and, 94
    communication, 53–56
    computers as, 48–49
    defined, 47
    digital books, 50
    planning, 33
    planning sheet, 185
    preparing, 43–45
    vendors, 51–53 (table)
    writing aids, 48–49
Thematic units
    activities structuring for, 36–37
    brought to life, 74, 75–76 (photo)
    checklist, 34
    choosing a book for, 25–26
    choosing a theme concept for, 23–25
    choosing vocabulary for, 28–29

classroom environment
    structure and, 36
concluding, 79–80
finalizing plans for, 29–30
games, 97–98
inclusion and, 100–102
individual goals in, 29
introduction, 57–59
language books for, 54–55
parent communication for, 31–33
planning, 18–19, 24–25, 119
planning sheets, 33
presentations, 77
program principles, 9–10
research on using, 7–8
scheduling events for, 30
team approach to, 14–18
virtual environments for,
    74, 75–76 (photo)
weekly lesson plan, 108–118
See also Instructional delivery
Theme Concept, 23
Themes Teachers Use, 7
Therapists 14, 29, 45
These Happy, Golden Years, 92
Three-legged easels, 45
Three Pigs, The, 20
Time for Kids, 69
Time for team planning, 17–18
Time/time clock/calendar skills, 105,
    112–113
Tornado in a bottle, 125–126
Touch screens, computer, 49
Transitions From Literature to Literacy, 20
Traumatic brain injury, 12
Tuck Everlasting, 25–26
Tutors, peer, 61, 102, 103 (photo)

Vanguard, 48
Vendors, technology, 51–53 (table)
Videos, 26, 56
Virtual environments, 74, 75–76 (photo)
Visual, 13, 22 (table), 28–30, 36, 41, 46, 62
Visual awareness, 22 (table)
Visual learning skills, 22 (table)
Vocabulary
    activity planning, 186
    cards, 128–131, 143–146, 156–160,
        167–171, 180–183
    choosing, 28–29
    games, 94–98, 110
    introducing, 59
    lesson plan, 110–111

teaching, 67–69
See also Language; Word(s)

Wagner, D. K., 43
Wagner, R., 50
Wakeman, S., 4
Walls, word, 65–66
Weather activities, 126–127
Web, planning, 26–28
Western Carolina University (WCU), 16
Westling, D., 13
Whale Rider, The, 74
Where the Lilies Bloom, 18, 20, 75 (photo)
    communication board, 161
    family tree activity, 150–151
    field trip, 153–155
    lesson plan, 148–161
    mountain views activity, 151–152
    parent letter, 152–153
    quilt day activity, 152–153
    stone soup activity, 153–155
    summary, 148
    theme plan, 149
    vocabulary, 156–160
White boards, 45, 115
Whole language, 3, 57
Winterling, V., 7
Wizard of Oz, The
    assessment, 92
    communication board, 184
    graphing skittles activity, 179
    individual journaling of, 86
    instructional delivery, 58, 68, 70
    lesson plan, 173–184

making roads activity, 176–177
poppies activity, 177–178
setting the stage, 40, 41 (photo), 42, 45
summary, 173–174
thematic unit, 28, 30
theme plan, 175
vocabulary, 180–183
Word(s)
    games, 94–98, 110
    meanings, 68
    symbol recognition, 67–68
    walls, 65–66
    See also Vocabulary
Writing
    aids, 48–49
    invitation, 115–116
    list making, 113
    mini lesson, 117
    predictable chart, 72–74, 114
    skills, 112–113, 115, 177
Writing With Symbols, 185
Written expression, 9, 16
    adaptive or assitive technology
        and, 49 (photo)
    assistive or adaptive
        technology and, 94
    challenges to, 22 (table)
    communication notebooks and, 53–55
    hands-on learning and, 42 (photo)
    individual goals and, 61
    invitations and, 115
    journaling and, 86 (photo)

Zygo Macaws, 44